T·H·E ANGRY MAN

David Stoop, Ph.D.
Stephen Arterburn, M.Ed.

WORD PUBLISHING
Dallas · London · Vancouver · Melbourne

The Angry Man
Copyright © 1991 Stephen Arterburn and David Stoop

Scripture quotations are from the Holy Bible, New International Version (NIV). Copyright © 1973, 1978, 1984 International Bible Society. Used by permission of Zondervan Bible Publishers.

The persons described in this book are composites drawn from the practices and research of Stephen Arterburn and David Stoop. Names and situations in all case studies have been altered to protect the privacy of individuals involved.

Library of Congress Cataloging-in-Publication Data

Arterburn, Stephen, 1953–
    The angry man : why does he act that way? / by Stephen Arterburn and David Stoop.
        p. cm.
    Includes bibliographical references.
    ISBN 0-8499-0779-9
    1. Anger. 2. Men — Psychology. 3. Masculinity (Psychology)
4. Interpersonal communication. I. Stoop, David A. II. Tile.
BF575.A5A77 1991
155.6 ' 32 — dc20   91 – 15148
                                                                      CIP

1 2 3 4 5 9 AGF 5 4 3
Printed in the United States of America

Dedication

To our wives, Jan and Sandy

Contents

Acknowledgments

When it came time to write together again, Joey Paul, at Word, asked if we were interested in writing about *The Angry Man*. Both of us have done a lot of work with men and with anger, so we said yes. This book is the result.

We want to thank Ed Stewart, for without his help, this book would probably still be an idea. We also want to thank Sally Masteller for helping us with the research and Melanie Grimes for making us readable.

Introduction

The Day
the Lawn Mower Died

Cliff was as kind and mild-mannered a husband and father as you'd ever want to meet. He worked hard, made a decent living, was active in his church, and loved to putter in his garden.

One summer day Cliff pulled his year-old power lawn mower out of the shed and rolled it onto his beautifully land-scaped back lawn. He attached the bagger, set the controls on "START," and pulled the cord. Nothing. He pulled again. The engine turned over a couple of times, coughed, then died. He pulled again, again, and again. With each vigorous pull of the cord the engine belched smoke and gas fumes but wouldn't start.

Finally, after another hearty pull, the engine roared to life. Cliff straightened up and adjusted the throttle, but before he could take a step the engine died again. He stared at the mower and sighed deeply. Then he tried to restart it—once, twice, three times—but it wouldn't kick in. After glaring at the mower for several seconds Cliff turned and walked toward the house.

Janice had noticed through the kitchen window that her husband was having trouble with the mower. "Is the mower broken?" she asked as Cliff walked in the back door and through the kitchen. He didn't answer her, didn't even acknowledge her presence. He just walked past her and down the hall to the den. In a couple of moments he came back through the kitchen carrying his prized deer-hunting rifle and a handful of shells. "Cliff?" Janice called to him in a tone of mild alarm. "Cliff, what are you doing?" Again Cliff walked past her and out the back door as if she were invisible. Janice held her breath as she watched him from the window.

Cliff walked to within ten feet of the lawn mower, then stopped. He methodically slid several shells into the rifle's magazine. Then he bolted a shell into the chamber, lifted the rifle, and took dead aim at the defenseless machine. *Pow — clang! Pow — clang! Pow — clang!* With each direct hit the lawn mower shuddered, and sparks and tiny shreds of metal exploded from it. It was a wonder that Cliff wasn't struck by the shrapnel.

After emptying the magazine into the lawn mower, Cliff calmly walked back into the house and retired to the den to clean his gun, closing the door behind him. Janice stood in the kitchen dumbfounded. She had never before seen such a change of character in her meek and mild husband. He was never one to display his emotions — until now! And it frightened her to wonder what other startling quirks might be lurking beneath Cliff's quiet, confident exterior.

The Phenomenon of Masculine Anger

You may think that Cliff's behavior is a little far-fetched for a healthy, mature, intelligent, American male, but it's really not. The description of Cliff's measured but violent assault on his stubborn lawn mower is based on a true case history. Cliff's explosion is representative of an alarmingly widespread phenomenon among men of the '90s. Men today are angry. Their anger is deep-seated and, like their other emotions, carefully guarded and controlled most of the time. They may not know why they're angry. They may even deny that they're angry. But they're ticked off, seething, boiling inside. And occasionally their anger bubbles menacingly to the surface as it did in Cliff that summer day.

Janice's surprise, concern, and fear at her husband's sudden, atypical behavior mirrors the emotional response of countless numbers of women who are coming face to face with the phenomenon of the angry man. "What's happened to him?" they cry to counselors across the land. "Was it something I did? Was it something I neglected to do? Is there any hope for him? For us?" Perhaps you've been asking some of these kinds of questions.

Like Cliff, the man who sleeps with you every night, bathes your children on Saturdays, and makes sure your car is gassed and lubed may be a smoldering volcano of anger ready to erupt when you least expect it. Perhaps you've already detected the rumbling. Perhaps he's already exploded in ways that have left you questioning, hurt, or feeling abandoned.

But unlike Cliff, your husband may not be ready to explode as obviously or as harmlessly as plugging the Lawn Boy with his Winchester thirty-aught-six. There are numerous and far more tragic ways — both subtle and blatant — that masculine anger can boil to the surface and cause harm:

• Fifty-two-year-old Brennan was a high-rolling electronics contractor in the aerospace industry. He worked 60 to 80 hours a week as a matter of course, and sometimes stayed at his office for days on end. Brennan provided his family with a magnificent home and plenty of money, and he gave generously to his church. At his wife's urging, Brennan exchanged his high-stress career for a financially comfortable early retirement. But he was soon bored with travel, golf, and gardening. So he bought another small company and plunged back into the only life he knew — incessant work. Eight months later Brennan dropped dead from a massive heart attack. Brennan was an angry man, and his anger-fueled workaholism resulted in his wife's becoming a young widow.

• At 38, Carlos is a husband, a father of twin daughters aged seven, and an assistant manager in a supermarket chain. Carlos has been with his company for 13 years, long enough to be promoted to manage a store of his own — his career goal. But it's obvious to him that the owners are hesitant to give full control of a store to a Hispanic. Carlos boasts to Manuela that he is the company's most loyal assistant manager, but she keeps urging him to go with another chain that will promote him.

Last month Manuela unexpectedly returned home early from a trip to her mother's and found Carlos in bed with their 15-year-old baby-sitter. Manuela was devastated. She told Carlos to pack his things and leave. After Carlos moved out, Manuela found several boxes of hard-core pornographic books and videos hidden in the attic. Carlos is an angry man, and his anger cost him his family.

• Vince was a successful real estate agent in the Houston area until a collapse in the housing market threatened him with financial ruin. He couldn't sell any of his properties, and his own plush home plummeted in value to 50 percent of what he had paid for it. Vince had built his business on his life's axiom: "If you just work hard enough and long enough, you will succeed." But he was working harder and longer than ever, and he was still failing. He grew increasingly depressed and angry at circumstances he couldn't control. Enid, his wife, felt him slipping away from her as a chasm widened between them. Soon she could no longer reach him.

• Marta had been ill for nearly two of the four years she and Kelvin had been married. Kelvin was attending seminary part-time and managing a small radio station near the school. He lived under the constant pressure of Marta's ill health, probation-status grades, and the radio station's solvency.

His classmates and coworkers often heard Kelvin claim that God would eventually deliver them from their stress-filled lifestyle. But the day after the seminary suspended him for poor grades and attendance, Kelvin plunged a hunting knife into Marta's chest, killing her, then slashed his wrists and bled to death. Kelvin was an angry man, and his anger left a painful scar on an entire community.

Although the circumstances and outcomes of these scenarios are vastly different, a common denominator exists: These men were angry, and their anger deeply hurt themselves and the women they loved.

Solution or Fantasy?

You may be thinking, "There are so many ways masculine anger can become harmful or destructive. How should a man deal with negative angry feelings to avoid these kinds of tragedies?"

To answer that, let's go back to Cliff and Janice several months before the incident in the back yard with the lawn mower and the deer rifle. Imagine the couple sitting alone in their favorite restaurant savoring the last bites of a delicious dinner. They've talked about many topics: their upcoming family vacation at the shore, the third-grade Sunday school class they teach together, and how they will spend a small inheritance from the estate of Janice's uncle who died last month.

The waiter has just refilled their coffee cups and cleared the table. Then Cliff launched into a topic that had been on his mind for several days: a lack of attention from Janice.

CLIFF: Honey, I have something else I want to talk to you about before we go home. I'm struggling with some personal feelings that I'm not sure how to deal with. If you don't mind, I'd like to tell you how I feel and hear your insights or opinions.

JANICE: Of course, Cliff. I always like it when you want to talk.

CLIFF: I've been a little lonely lately. It seems that with both of us working and the kids involved in so many activities, we don't get the time alone together that I would like. This is the first time in months that we've been able to eat at a restaurant that doesn't have a kids' menu! The whole thing kind of came to a head for me last Thursday night. When I got home from work I wanted to sit down with you and talk about the day. But we were interrupted three times by Peter wanting help with his math homework.

Then you and Mindy had to leave for children's choir practice before we were done with dinner. And after the kids went to bed I felt abandoned when you spent 45 minutes on the phone with one of your clients. By then we were both too tired for much conversation, let alone sex. Maybe I'm a little self-centered, Janice, but I feel angry when I don't receive the attention I want and need. I'm just sorry that I didn't bring it up sooner.

JANICE: I'm glad you could tell me that, Cliff. I sensed that Thursday night was a problem for you, and I'm sorry that I was so occupied. I cherish our one-on-one times, too.

CLIFF: Then let's talk about setting aside some special time just for us. And while we talk, let's share a piece of chocolate mousse cake. Waiter!

Does this tender little vignette sound like it came right out of Fantasyland? Well, you're right; it never happened. If it had, an innocent Lawn Boy mower may have been spared a brutal and untimely death. And, more seriously, had Brennan been able to talk about his anger-driven workaholism at the beginning of his career, he may have lived to enjoy retirement with his wife. Had Carlos been able to verbalize his resentment over his employer's discrimination, he may not have been drawn into the sexual trap that threatened to end his marriage. Had Vince shared his depression and anger with Enid, they might have been able to bridge the gap that his failure opened between them. And had Kelvin been honest about the fears and failures that stalked him, perhaps he and Marta would be working together today in a radio station or a church as they dreamed of doing.

The first step in resolving masculine anger is a man's willingness and ability to talk about what's bugging him. But that's precisely why the conversation above sounds like it came from the lips of Ward and June Cleaver, the perfect, problem-free parents in TV's classic *"Leave It to Beaver"* series. Most men in the real world are neither willing nor able to talk about what's bothering them. Part I of this book explores the reasons behind this reticence and the often tragic results that accompany it.

Today's man is caught between a rock and a hard place. His anger boils inside him, and his relationships, his job, even his health and his life may be in jeopardy because of it. But he can't find peace because he can't or won't bring his feelings to the surface, talk about them, and resolve them.

A lot of women wonder if they can help their husbands resolve their anger and find peace. We're not talking about mothering him, pressuring him, cajoling him, or nagging him out of his anger. Taking that approach is like trying to douse a fire with kerosene. Nor is this book written to simply help you live with your angry husband by learning to just hunker down, bite the bullet, and "take it." Rather, you will learn some practical steps to better understand him, helping him become aware of his anger, expressing it in a positive, healthy way, and resolving his troubling feelings. Part II discusses several key tips you can employ to help your husband find peace through anger awareness, expression, and resolution.

Think about It, Talk about It with Him

1. Has your husband had some kind of a "lawn mower experience" — an occasion when he displayed his feelings in a startling way? Describe.

2. To what degree do you feel that he has his anger under control? Circle the word you feel is most appropriate.

Always   Often   Sometimes   Seldom   Never

3. How do you know when he is angry?

4. How often do you feel responsible for his feelings or outbursts of anger?

Always   Often   Sometimes   Seldom   Never

5. How has his anger hurt you in the past?

PART I

Why Men Are Angry and What They Do When They Are

1

Growing Up without Father

Experts are discovering that a primary source of the seething undercurrent of anger that pervades much of the male population is the diminishing influence of the father in a man's life. A number of studies in recent years have shown that less than one percent of males have or have had a close relationship with their fathers. Many men cannot remember their fathers touching them affectionately or telling them, "I love you." Men often are not very emotional, but if you want to see a man get emotional, just ask him about his father. A large number of adult males today have grown up virtually without their fathers, and they are hurt and angry because of it.

What happened to the father-son relationship to create such a negative response in men? Perhaps a couple of examples will illustrate the origin and extent of the problem.

It's So Nice to Have a Man around the House

Farrell Courtney lives with his wife Eva and their four children on a moderate-sized farm in Nebraska. Despite the industrialization that is gradually "modernizing" faraway cities like New York, Chicago, and San Francisco, the Courtneys are a typical family in 1895. They grow wheat and raise chickens to sell or trade for supplies. They own a couple of sturdy horses to pull plows and wagons. They tend three cows for milk and butter and a large garden that supplies them with fresh seasonal vegetables and herbs.

Before their children came along, Farrell and Eva worked the farm together with Farrell's father, Jeb. But now with two daughters aged two and four, and two sons aged seven and ten, Eva spends most of her time baking, cooking, and tending the young ones. And Jeb, who raised Farrell on the same spread, is able to do less and less of the hard labor. So the young Courtney boys, Joshua and Adam, have replaced their mother and grandfather in the field as Farrell's chief farm hands.

Almost since they could walk, Joshua and Adam have worked with their father. They rise before sunup seven days a week to milk the cows and herd them to pasture. Depending on the season, they may spend the day plowing, seeding, cultivating, or harvesting. When they aren't tending the wheat, they're weeding the vegetable garden, building a new chicken coop, stacking hay, cleaning stalls, mending fences, or one of dozens of chores which need to be done to keep the farm operating.

Joshua and Adam spend a few hours each day at the school house, but their real education about life and being a man in the 1890s comes from their pa. He teaches them about the weather, agriculture, and commerce as they work the soil from plowing and planting through harvest and distribution. Using the farm animals as curriculum, he teaches them about life, growth, and death—including the details of sex, reproduction, birth, and infant care. He models for them the qualities of initiative, diligence, and perseverance in their work.

The boys learn how to be tender and protective by watching Pa care for their mother and sisters. And when work, weather, and school permit, Farrell and his sons hunt, fish, swim, and ride together, where there is plenty of time for talk and play.

Farrell Courtney is the primary mentor, guide, counselor, and friend in his sons' lives. As Joshua and Adam grow into adolescence and young manhood, Farrell will accept them as full partners in the farm, just as Farrell's father did with him. The three men will expand their farm by claiming more of the adjoining prairie. Joshua and Adam and their families will take over the farm as Farrell and Eva age and eventually die. It has been this way in the Courtney family for generations.

The Making of an Angry Man

Now let's race ahead in time from 1895 to 1955 and look in on the family of Bill Courtney, the adult son of Adam Courtney, who was born in 1918. Like an increasing number of Americans, many of the descendants of Farrell and Eva Courtney migrated from rural Nebraska to the urban centers of the nation. Bill Courtney left the family farm in the '30s for a lucrative job in Omaha repairing farm machinery. After serving in World War II, Bill settled in suburban Los Angeles, married, and began working as a machinist at an aircraft plant.

On a typical day in 1955, Bill rises early each morning, gulps down a cup of coffee, and leaves the house by 6:30 A.M. Liz Courtney gets nine-year-old Bobby and six-year-old Beth up and ready for school and helps them with their homework in the afternoon. At 5:00 P.M. Bill arrives home from work. The family hurries through dinner in order to watch television until Bobby and Beth's bedtime. Liz tucks them in, hears their prayers, and kisses them good night while Bill spins the channels looking for a baseball game or a boxing match.

Bill plays golf every Saturday morning and tinkers with the car the rest of the day. If Bobby is lucky, his dad will play catch with him for a half-hour before dark. Then Bill will treat the family to a drive-in movie, hot dogs, and popcorn — unless he's playing cards with his buddies, as he does one or two Saturdays a month.

After church on Sunday, Bobby and Beth may be able to talk their dad into a game of Monopoly before he retires to the hammock for his afternoon nap. And on Sunday night the Courtneys watch TV, then retire early so they can start the cycle all over again on Monday morning.

In contrast to his Grandpa Adam at the same age, Bobby spends most of his waking hours at home with his mother, not his father. Apart from school, most of what Bobby learns about life, work, and people comes from his mother's instruction and example because she's home and Bill's not. Bobby is substantially deprived of the fatherly instruction, guidance, counsel, and friendship that his grandfather received as a boy. Bobby will soon be a man. But his limited interaction and experience with his father has provided him little understanding about what a man is or does.

In 1963 17-year-old Bobby prepares to graduate from high school. As he stands on the brink of adulthood, he's confused and apprehensive about the future. He doesn't know what he wants to do, or what he's able to do, for a career. Bill wants him to follow in his footsteps to become a machinist. But Bobby barely knows what a machinist does, since he's only visited his father at work a few times.

One of Bobby's teachers tells him that he is blessed with a sharp mind, and that he could make a lot of money as an attorney. With little direction to go on, young Bob follows his teacher's suggestion and, after college, graduates from law school. As always, Liz Courtney encourages Bob in his endeavors, but Bill shows little interest in his son's chosen field. Feeling restless and unfulfilled, Bob flits between a number of law firms over 15 years. Thinking a change of scene might help, Bob moves his wife and children to Seattle and opens a small private practice.

Today Bob is out of law and owns a small boat repair shop on Puget Sound. His restlessness and dissatisfaction with life has strained his marriage. He pours all his energies into boats and sailing. His children see very little of him.

The Disappearing American Father

The stark contrast between the Courtney families of the nineteenth and twentieth centuries illustrates the major cause of masculine anger in our generation. The American father has all but disappeared from the family. Change the names and dates in the family history of Bob Courtney and you likely have a picture of the man in your life. Like Bill's son, he probably grew up with a father who worked outside the home and provided limited influence, instruction, friendship, and guidance to his son.

At the same time, boys like Bobby long for their fathers. They dress like him and want to act like him. They beg their fathers to teach them how to do "men" things like throw balls, be in the outdoors, or fix things. And with their dads missing in action in their lives, many boys grow up with those yearnings and needs unfulfilled.

Consequently, a man today may have approached manhood feeling unprepared and ill-equipped for life as a man. He knew little about how a man works, plays, relates, or loves because the one man he should learn the most from was largely absent during his critical developmental years. He is trying to conquer the world as his father did but struggles because Dad never showed him how to do it.

The Downside of the Revolution

What happened to our nation's fathers and sons in the decades between Farrell Courtney in Nebraska and Bill Courtney in Los Angeles? Actually, the difference between these two fathers has its roots in the Industrial Revolution of the eighteenth and nineteenth centuries and the transition between an agrarian society and an industrial society in our country.

Like the majority of American men, Farrell Courtney was born and raised in a primarily agrarian society. Fathers and sons lived and worked together on the family farm. Those men who didn't farm labored at trades that their sons learned from them through years of observation, instruction, and hands-on experience. By and large, the sons of farmers became farmers, the sons of blacksmiths became blacksmiths, the sons of merchants became merchants, and so on. Boys spent most of their time with their fathers, who were their primary mentors.

But as the industrialization of our nation expanded, more and more men were needed to build and repair the machines, sell and deliver the products, count the profits, and pay the bills.

Increasing numbers of ambitious men like Bill Courtney, Farrell's grandson, moved to the city to take these jobs. Instead of spending the day tutoring their sons in the skills of life and work, these men left home every morning to pursue their careers at the factory, shop, or office—and their sons stayed home with their mothers. The more time and energy a man directed to his work away from home, the less time he had to spend mentoring his sons.

Severing the Extended Family

Our nation's sons lost more than their fathers during the industrialization of the twentieth century. They also lost a most viable alternative for masculine input—their grandfathers. Indeed, when a man uprooted his family to take a job in a distant city or state, he likely detached his children from a large and nurturing extended family. In the agrarian society a boy commonly enjoyed daily interaction with not only his father but with his grandfather, uncles, brothers, and cousins. His male kinfolk were his coworkers, his teachers, and his best friends. They worked together, ate together, and played together. Moving away from this network seriously reduced the flow of necessary masculine nurture and influence in a boy's life.

By the end of World War II, Bill, Liz, Bobby, and Beth Courtney characterized the typical American family. A father's work was outside the home, consuming his primary interests and energies. His physical, educational, emotional, and spiritual input to his son was largely incidental, limited to his "free time" — i.e., those few hours or minutes in his week when he wasn't at work, traveling to or from work, or recuperating from work. And the vital nurture of a loving grandfather was often also absent due to great distance between him and his grandson.

Father-to-son influence was defaulted to mothers, teachers, coaches, pastors, and youth workers — all noble but inferior substitutes.

Like Bob Courtney in our story, today's men are often restless and off-center for lack of a father/mentor in their lives. Men aren't just looking for someone to teach them a trade; they're starving for masculine emotional input. They sense a deep need for affirmation and validation from a man who loves them and is committed to them. And this gnawing void has given rise to a generation of angry men.

The Irresponsible Father

Several other levels of fallout from the industrialization of America have further distanced fathers from their sons and contributed to the anger they feel. Numbers of men today grew up in homes where the father was completely absent by reason of divorce. In many cases these men judged their roles as husbands and fathers to be expendable in the pursuit of their careers and lifestyles. At some point their sons had to deal with the shocking reality that "Daddy doesn't want to live with us anymore." A boy's feeling of disapproval from his father's departure may cause him to spend his life seeking the acceptance, love, and approval of his father.

When fathers abandon their families, they often plant seeds of discord in their sons that may unconsciously come to the surface in the sons' marriages. Boys still perceive their fathers as the epitome of masculinity even if the father has little time or care for his sons. In an attempt to get the father's approval the son may unconsciously repeat the father's behavior thinking that will get the attention and approval he craves.

In other families, fathers remained in the home physically but abandoned their sons emotionally. These men worked day and night, and then played hard all weekend—shirking any responsibility for their families beyond providing the rent and groceries. Not only was the father-son relationship void of nurture, it left a negative impact on the boy, who was treated as an inconvenience or an interruption in his father's life. Just at the time the boy needed a man to help him practice being a man, his father was off somewhere struggling with his own manhood.

Then there's the abusive father. Some men grew up with fathers who abused them physically, emotionally, and/or sexually. These fathers went out of their way to ruin their sons' lives.

Experience has shown us that the men who are happiest and most content in the masculine role today are those whose fathers invested a great deal of time and energy in their lives. These dads may have worked outside the home, as the vast majority of fathers in our society today do. But they were committed to maintaining a positive, nurturing relationship with their sons. These fathers supported their sons in their chosen careers, attempted to understand their ambitions (even when they differed from their own), and appreciated their achievements. As a result of their investment, their sons are among the most well-adjusted and peaceful husbands and fathers in our society.

However, men with these kinds of fathers are in the minority today. Most men are struggling to recover from relationships with fathers who failed to nurture, affirm, and validate them at some level. These fathers have left their sons a legacy of pain, confusion, frustration, anxiety, bitterness, fear, and anger. These adult sons are the angry men of our society. It's possible that your man may be among them.

When Does a Boy Become a Man?

Another reason men in our culture grope angrily through manhood is the absence of a identifiable rite of passage. They are not confident in their masculinity because their fathers didn't tell them when boyhood ended and manhood began, nor did their fathers celebrate the event. Many cultures around the world designate a specific year in a boy's life when the men in his family or tribe induct him into manhood with great ceremony. Sometimes the boy leaves his mother's hut at this time and moves in with the men of the tribe.

Sometimes the boy's body is permanently scarred in some way to signify the passing from boyhood to manhood. There's an African tribe where, on the day of induction, one of the boy's adult teeth is knocked out. From that day forward, every time he sticks his tongue through that hole he is reminded that he is a man. Males who still have that tooth act and are treated like boys. Males who have lost that tooth act and are treated like men. The induction ceremony is often painful and frightening for an adolescent boy. But afterward he flaunts his painful wounds as proud medals of his manhood.

An old American Indian legend describes a similar rite of passage. During the winter of induction, a boy was taken to a frozen lake. A hole was cut in the ice, and the boy dived to the bottom of the lake three times. Each time he surfaced he had to bring up a stone or other object to prove he had been to the bottom. From that day onward, he carried those three tokens in a pouch around his neck as tangible proof that he was a man.

No such rite of passage exists in our culture. Furthermore, the fathers of today's men were probably so busy just trying to be men that they didn't even think of preparing their sons for manhood. And today's men are confused, frustrated, and angry as a result.

The Women in a Man's Life

Back in the 1890s, Eva Courtney certainly contributed significantly to the mental, emotional, and social development of her sons, Joshua and Adam. But, in reality, her contribution was largely complementary to the substantive input they received from Farrell, their father and mentor. After all, a woman can teach her son many things, but only a man can teach a boy how to be a man. Farrell Courtney is an excellent example of the father/mentor which characterized a less industrialized America.

By contrast, Bill Courtney reflects the twentieth-century caricature of the career-oriented father who has abdicated the mentoring of his son Bobby to Liz, his wife. She wakes him up, prepares him for school, helps him with his homework, drives him to Little League practice (Bill does try to get to his games!), and puts him to bed at night. To his credit, at least Bill is still in the home and relatively supportive. But he is definitely second-string to Liz in the area of providing nurture and emotional input to young Bobby.

More Than a Mother's Love

Mothers are wonderful, and you'll be hard-pressed to find an adult son who doesn't love and appreciate his mother immensely. But a boy's successful development requires the substantial, positive masculine influence of a father/mentor. As Dr. Frank Pittman, a psychiatrist specializing in the treatment of men, asserts:

> A mother may give her son booming self-esteem, may imbue him with a wonderful sense of his specialness, but she can't have expertise on what he as a man is to do with that masculine specialness. Mothers, no matter how wise and wonderful, can

only point boys in certain directions, but boys need
fathers to show them how far they should go. . . .
It's hard to imagine how we can raise a better generation of sons until we have a better generation of
fathers.[1]

When a father's influence is weak or missing for any of
the reasons detailed above, the strong, compensating feminine influence can cause some problems in a boy's development. Since his self-concept is not being shaped by the man
in his life, he will either pattern himself after his mother or
try to be just the opposite of her. A boy may fear that his
mother will stifle his developing masculinity, that she will
domesticate the wild, conquering animal he knows he must
be. Growing up as a male with a female as primary mentor
can lead to role confusion. In the main, these men are the Bob
Courtneys of our society — wandering through life anxious
and frustrated in search of a father/mentor to validate them
as men, husbands, and fathers.

A man's boyhood relationship with his mother profoundly affects the kind of woman he looks for in a wife. If
his relationship with his mother was one of fear because of
overdependence on either one's part, he will likely try to find
someone different from her. He will especially avoid women
with traits that made his mother a threat to him in some way.
However, if a man's mother made him feel secure and proud
in his masculinity, he will look for a woman to marry who
has his mother's affirming traits.

To further muddle the psyches of men who grew up with
an overbalanced feminine influence, the feminist movement
has redefined womanhood in our culture. A man's female
peers come across as stronger, more assertive, and more
dominant than his mother ever was. Most men, especially
those without a strong father/mentor, don't know how to
respond to today's woman.

Coping without Father

Underneath Bob Courtney's strong, together exterior as a successful Los Angeles attorney and Seattle businessman is a frightened little boy who is still desperately searching for affirmation and validation as a man. That's where a lot of men live today. Being unsure of how to carry off the masculine role, they hide their fears behind masks of strength because that's what their fathers did. But when that facade is threatened on the job or in the home, the cornered little boy lashes out in anger.

What can be done to help him? How can we as a culture help men resolve the anger that the absence of the strong father/mentor has produced?

Men Talking to Men

One hopeful sign in society is the growth of a men's movement. Just as the women's movement has brought women together and helped them clarify their identity and role in the world, so the men's movement is helping angry men heal masculine loneliness, unscramble their role confusion, and come to terms with their need for validation as men.

The beginnings of a men's movement surfaced in the early 1980s in response to a call issued by poet Robert Bly. A burly, silver-haired man, in his mid-60s described as a cross between Garrison Keillor and Zeus, Bly challenges men to put down their competitive swords and shields and find their common ground of loneliness, hurt, and abandonment. He and others began sharing stories and ideas with other men at poetry readings and eventually on weekend and week-long retreats.

Today, Bly, along with storyteller and philosopher Michael Meade, psychologist James Hillman, and others, draws sellout crowds around the country. One men-only retreat they hosted attracted over 700 men, and many retreats turn away hundreds. Bly's call in these gatherings is for men to examine how the conditioning they received as boys is sabotaging their lives as men by leading them to distrust other men and ask too much from the women in their lives.

Many men would respond positively to the opportunity to attend a men-only retreat that deals with the critical issues of masculinity and the missing father. If such an event is available in your area, think about recommending it to your husband.

Dealing with the Loss

To some degree, the angry man has lost his father. It may be an emotional loss, as it was for Bob Courtney whose father didn't adequately fulfill the role of father/mentor in his life. It may also be a physical loss, as with a father who dies leaving no hope that the father/son relationship will be restored.

As with any loss in life, men experiencing a sense of loss in their relationship with their fathers must grieve that loss. Without proper, healthy grieving the inner hurt is like an open sore, vulnerable to repeated pain and infection. A man must deal with the losses in his life, or he will never be at peace with himself or his world.

Being a True Friend

The greatest asset to a hurting, angry man is a faithful, loving friend, someone who will understand him and stand with him as he rediscovers his masculinity. Part II will help you develop your role as a true friend.

Throughout history, men have been hunters. Initially they hunted because they needed the meat to survive. In some corners of the world this is still true, but not in our culture. Yet all men still seem to have a need to search, discover, and conquer. Some go deer-hunting just for the adventure of stalking, and they call the trip a success even if they don't bag a buck. They sometimes get so excited at discovering a deer in the wild that they can't hold their rifles steady to get off a shot. They call it "buck fever." And they love to conquer, as evidenced by the way they stuff and mount dead animal heads in their homes.

The rewards of searching for, discovering, and conquering wild animals are fleeting. Why? Because in a sense men are really searching for themselves. Finding and killing a deer only anesthetizes the gnawing need for a moment. They will be back up in the woods next year just as determined as ever.

Think about It, Talk about It with Him

1. Did your husband grow up with a father more like Farrell Courtney or Bill Courtney? In what way was his father like either (or both) man (men)?

2. How do his current relationship with or feelings about his father reflect his boyhood relationship with his father?

3. Could his father be classified as an irresponsible father in some significant way? If so, explain.

4. How would you judge the overall impact and influence of these men in his life?

Father:	Terrible	Poor	Average	Good	Excellent
Grandfathers:	Terrible	Poor	Average	Good	Excellent
Uncles:	Terrible	Poor	Average	Good	Excellent
Older brothers:	Terrible	Poor	Average	Good	Excellent

5. Do you agree that the feminist movement has contributed to the confusion men experience while attempting to validate their masculinity? Why or why not?

2

Trying to Live Up
to a Myth

It began almost before we were aware that boys and girls were
different at all. The adults in our lives quizzed us as little
tykes: "What are little boys and girls made of?" And we
proudly answered with the lines drummed into us by Mom
and Dad, grandparents, aunts and uncles, and teachers: "Little
girls are made of sugar and spice and everything nice. Little
boys are made of snips and snails and puppy-dog tails."

We learned very early in life that girls are supposed to
be soft and warm and boys are supposed to be rough and
tumble. Girls play house and receive dolls as Christmas gifts.
Boys play war and get toy guns, tanks, and planes. When little
girls get hurt by their playmates, they run home crying to
Mommy. But when little boys get punched, they punch back.
Teenage girls have slumber parties so they can spend hours
talking about parents and boys. But teenage boys get together

to race their motorcycles or cars, pound each other on the football field, or boast about their romantic conquests.

By the time we reach adulthood we are thoroughly indoctrinated and well-practiced in our culture's expectations of what men and women are supposed to be. According to the traditional sex roles, women are affectionate, gentle, kind, expressive, relational, emotional, understanding, submissive, passive, and nurturing. Men, of course, are different — at least that's what we've been told ever since we learned to recite "sugar and spice and everything nice" and "snips and snails and puppy-dog tails." The traditional male is characterized as adventurous, achievement-oriented, assertive, autonomous, dominant, confident, practical, unemotional, and strong. As in childhood, women are supposed to be soft and warm, and men are supposed to be rough and tumble.

Furthermore, there is an incredibly powerful cultural pressure on men to be "masculine," even though most of that pressure is only perceived. Dr. Frank Pittman colorfully describes this pressure:

> As a guy develops and practices his masculinity, he is accompanied and critiqued by an invisible male chorus of all the other guys who hiss or cheer as he attempts to approximate the masculine ideal, who push him to sacrifice more and more of his humanity for the sake of his masculinity, and who ridicule him when he holds back. The chorus is made up of all the guy's comrades and rivals, all his buddies and bosses, his male ancestors and his male cultural heroes, his models of masculinity — and above all, his father, who may have been a real person in the boy's life, or may have existed for him only as the myth of the man who got away.[1]

From this invisible male chorus a man feels pressured to live up to a code of conduct that requires him to maintain masculine attitudes and behaviors (however they are defined) at all times and in all places.

Playing the Role

But is that the way it really is? Are these traditional sex roles reflective of genuine genetic differences? Or do men and women behave differently because we are literally playing sex "roles" — performing unwritten scripts produced and directed by the culture in which we were raised? In other words, are men really rough and tumble, or do they just act that way because our culture has told them that's how you act when you're made of snips and snails and puppy-dog tails?

Most experts in human behavior reject the king-of-the-mountain (and king of his woman) male image of the past. Sure, men and women are different anatomically, and there may be other gender-related differences. But, as psychologist Sidney Jourard contended, men and women have the same basic psychological needs, such as the need to know and be known by others, the need to be mutually interdependent, the need to love and be loved, and the need to find purpose and meaning in life.[2] In reality, underneath our cultural costumes, men and women are more alike than they are different.

But the different roles we play as men and women profoundly affect the degree to which our common needs are met. By reason of the softness and warmth they have practiced since childhood, women are more open and relational — qualities that are conducive to inner needs being met. However, rough and tumble little boys often grow up to be men who are closed and competitive in their relationships. Men would be better off if they exercised some of the qualities that have been culturally designated to the feminine role. Yet men resist appearing affectionate, gentle, kind, expressive, relational, emotional, understanding, submissive, passive, and nurturing for fear they will be judged less than manly. Many of them feel that the women's movement left them looking and feeling too wimpy.

They want some of the World War II, John Wayne hardness back in their lives. After all, this is the land where men are men and women are women, or at least that's how the myth goes.

Here then is another source of masculine anger. Men are trying to live out the stereotypical role of being rough and tumble, self-sufficient, and independent, and in so doing many of their basic needs are going unmet. Conversely, if a man opens himself to others in order to meet his inner needs, he may think of himself or be thought of by others as unmanly. He's in a double bind. And the result is discontent and frustration that can easily degenerate into anger.

The Myths of Masculinity

Parents prepare their boys to charge into the world, take care of themselves, compete with the other men, take control, and find women who will take care of them. They feel they must succeed at these tasks if they are to become men. But when men succeed too well for too long, they develop what Dr. Pittman calls "mascupathology." An example of mascupathology is the way men treat women differently from the way they treat each other. Mascupaths do so to the extreme. Enchanted by their own masculinity, mascupaths have trouble getting comfortable with women. They are tense and on guard, and they don't let down their masculine anger. They are so intent on displaying their gender before the opposite sex that they can't seem to be friends with women. This may be why the friendship you have longed for with your man has seemed so unattainable.

If an angry man is going to find peace with himself, you both need to understand his mascupathology, the cultural myths of masculinity that may be blocking him from fulfilling his basic needs. If he doesn't understand this conflict between myth and reality and demythologize his masculinity, his anger will eventually become destructive. Let's look at a number of myths that tend to perpetuate masculine anger.

I Am What I Do

Have you ever listened to men introduce themselves to each other for the first time?

"Hi, my name is Jack Dixon."

"Good to meet you, Jack. I'm Ken Edwards."

"What do you do, Ken?"

"I manage Wilson's Hardware Store here in town. And you, Jack?"

"Senior design engineer with Allied Electronics."

One of the primary myths of masculinity is that a man's identity is based on what he does or accomplishes, principally his job slot or career path. That's why men meeting each other often share names and job descriptions in the same breath. That's why men are often so achievement-oriented. That's also why men are so despondent, sometimes even suicidal, when their business falls apart, when they fail to gain the promotion they've strived for, or when they can't hold down a job.

Our culture has trained men that their accomplishments, especially in the world of employment, are their credentials for manhood. To many men, if they're a failure at what they do, they're a failure at being a man.

Yet in reality, a man's identity (as well as a woman's) is based on who he is apart from what he does. Identity is a matter of character, not accomplishment, a matter of being and relating, not doing. This is apparent in the call of Jesus Christ to His disciples, as recorded in the Bible in Mark 3:14: "He appointed twelve—designating them apostles—that they might be with him and that he might send them out to preach and to have authority to drive out demons."

Notice that Jesus definitely called the apostles to *do something:* to preach the gospel and drive out demons. But His first call was for them to *be someone*—His men. He wanted a mutually loving, nurturing, caring relationship with these men.

Christ's acceptance and approval of His disciples was always based on the being part of discipleship, not the doing part. The disciples enjoyed some successes in their mission. But they also experienced some failures, particularly during Christ's arrest, trial, and crucifixion when "all the disciples deserted him and fled" (Matthew 26:56). Had the disciples based their identity on their performance, they would have reason to consider themselves failures.

But after His resurrection, Jesus didn't reprimand them for what they did or didn't do. Instead He met privately with them several times before His ascension to assure them that they were still His men. Then He gave them the Great Commission (Matthew 28:16-20), and the disciples successfully carried it out because they had a firm grasp on their identity in Christ.

Similarly, today a man needs to understand that the essence of his identity is more than what he creates, designs, produces, sells, or repairs. The doing part of his life — job, advancement, success, recognition — is secondary to the being part. The more he focuses on who he is, the better he will be able to handle his failures and the pressures to succeed he feels in what he does.

The epitome of the I-am-what-I-do syndrome among today's men is the workaholic. Workaholics often accept this title as a badge of honor. In their eyes they are more manly than other men because they accomplish more in their 80-hour week than the sloths who only punch a clock for 40 hours a week.

That's all part of the myth. Workaholism is nothing more than busy work. Sometimes it produces money, sometimes is doesn't. Money isn't the issue. The real goal of the workaholic is to stay so busy that he doesn't have to deal with the inner pain of unmet basic needs. It's a vicious cycle. He throws himself into his work to find fulfillment. But his work cuts him off from those who nurture and affirm him as a person. In response, he just works longer and harder, further distancing himself from the being and relating part of his life.

Workaholics don't want to deal with a nagging wife, disobedient kids, increasing crime and pollution in their town, war, etc. So instead of looking within themselves for the resources to deal with these things, they get busy. And if they don't get busy, they get drunk, they hit someone, or they have an affair — all because they are so focused on what they must do instead of on what they must be.

Focus on Being

How can a man break through this myth and begin to see value in his identity and his relationships? He must start relating to people — especially other men — apart from what he does. Men need to open up their schedules, set aside their Day-Timers, and get to the business of finding out who they are.

Nathan meets each week with a group of four other men to do what men rarely do. They purposely avoid talking about what they do in order to talk about who they are and how they feel. They're learning to peel away the layers of the ingrained masculine facade. They're learning to be transparent with each other about their fears and insecurities. And they're learning to give and receive the nurture, affirmation, and encouragement they each desperately need but are often too "manly" to seek.

For example, recently Nathan exposed to his four friends an area of inner pain. "My father is in a nursing home," he began. "He's totally incapacitated. His mind is gone. I went to dress him and take care of him on Father's Day, but I could hardly hold myself together. I keep wishing that he will come out of his mental fog and tell me just once before he dies, 'You are a good son.' But I know he never will." Nathan was on the verge of tears.

The other men in the group leaned in to comfort Nathan with their hands on his shoulder (something "real" men don't do!). "If he knew you as we know you, and if he were able to speak, Nate," one man said, "he *would* say it."

"Yes, Nathan," added another, "you *are* a good son."

There aren't many men who function together as these five men function. It's such a radical break from the pervading myth that exalts doing over being. If a man doesn't have such a group, you end up being the primary source of validation, affirmation, and encouragement for the primary being side of his life. He needs more than just you.

When your man stops focusing on doing the best job an attorney, salesman, or assembler can do and starts focusing on being the best man he can be, he will discover that he will be an even better attorney, salesman, or assembler. Encouraging him as a person and a man apart from what he does is a key to this transition.

I Am What I Earn

For most men in our society, the score card for success in what they do is the monthly paycheck, and the trophies of success are the grown-up "toys" their earnings can purchase for them. This myth, which tempts men to base their self-worth on the money and material goods they can accumulate, is an extension of the I- am-what-I-do myth. The man trapped in this cultural delusion thinks, "If I can just work a little harder and longer this year, I'll be able to upgrade my lease car to a BMW, and I will be a success."

The I-am-what-I-earn myth explodes in the light of reports from psychologists and counselors that the wealthiest men in society are often also the angriest. Studies show that unbridled greed leads to unbridled hostility in men. When he doesn't have enough, he's angry because he can't buy all the toys he wants. And when he has more than he needs, he's angry because the toys don't bring him the fulfillment he seeks, so he grabs for even more. And each new assault on the elusive goal of financial independence simply deters the angry man from coming to terms with who he is apart from what he can accumulate.

As Jesus suggests, this anger-breeding myth is defused when a man learns to focus on life instead of money and possessions: "Do not worry about your life, what you will eat or drink; or about your body, what you will wear. Is not life more important than food, and the body more important than clothes?" (Matthew 6:25).

Furthermore, the sooner a man becomes satisfied with what he has and stops comparing his financial score card and trophies with those of other men, the better he will feel about himself. The apostle Paul states: "I have learned to be content whatever the circumstances. I know what it is to be in need, and I know what it is to have plenty. I have learned the secret of being content in any and every situation, whether well fed or hungry, whether living in plenty or in want" (Philippians 4:11-12). Men who opt to be satisfied with what they possess will have more time and energy for the kinds of nurturing relationships that will meet their basic needs.

Your attitude toward money and possessions can either fuel or cool your man's anger in this area. If you have trouble living within your means, you may simply help to drive him to earn more just to keep you happy. However, the more you can do to promote an atmosphere of contentment for what you have, the less pressure he may feel to earn and spend.

Real Men Always Have Great Sex

This myth is widely accepted because of the strong support it gains in the media, particularly television and films. The man on the screen is ready for sex at the slightest sign of female interest, regardless of what he may be doing at the moment. And his sexual encounters always result in an earth-shaking climax for him and his woman. Any man in the media who turns down a sexual invitation no matter how subtle is portrayed as weird, unmanly, or latently gay.

The media's depiction of sex comes straight out of Fantasyland. In the real world, a man's readiness for sex with his wife can be dampened by a number of factors: illness, a bad day at work, a good football game on TV, or a number of other distractions. The man who compares his off-and-on sex drive to the "always ready, willing, and able" status of the "studs" on the screen may panic. "What's wrong with me?" he agonizes. "Friday I told her to wait until after the game. Tonight I'm too tired. Am I becoming impotent?"

The myth of the perpetually sexual male promotes deep feelings of inadequacy in men. And when they feel inadequate and out of control in the sexual area, they are going to be angry. Some of the most violent men psychologists counsel are severely sexually impaired for some reason.

In order to defuse the anger of perceived sexual inadequacy in your man, affirm him where he is adequate while resisting the temptation to criticize him where he may be having difficulty. For example, if he isn't very gentle during lovemaking, instead of criticizing him for it, look for the most gentle thing he does and praise him for that fleeting act of gentleness. Harping at your man for being too insensitive, too tired, or whatever only deepens his frustration and anger.

If you are both willing, attend a workshop on intimacy or sexual compatibility in order to improve your lovemaking skills. The more confidence a man can develop in his sexual ability, and the more he realizes the fallacy of the male sexual myth, the better he will feel about himself and the less anger he will experience in this area.

Men Must Always Be Strong

The male sex role stereotype demands that men be healthy, strong, and self-sufficient in every way. Any admission of weakness is seen as a compromise of manliness. This is no more obvious than in the realm of physical health. In his article, "Myths of Masculinity: Impact upon Men's Health," Dr. David Forrester, associate professor of nursing at Pace University in New York, notes several significant facts that reflect the myth that men feel they must always be physically strong:

• Studies show that, by 6 years of age, boys perceive themselves to be less vulnerable to illness and tougher than girls.
• Men experience more accidental injuries, coronary artery disease, emphysema, hernia, and peptic ulcers than women.

- Men die more frequently than women from malignant neoplasm of the respiratory system, bronchitis, emphysema, asthma, chronic ischemic heart disease, acute myocardial infarction, and cirrhosis of the liver.
- A higher proportion of men suffer from physical activity limitations due to chronic conditions.
- Men engage in more physical activities and behaviors characterized by risk taking, aggression, and violence, contributing to the higher incidence of accidents, suicide, and homicide among men.
- The average woman will outlive the average man by seven to eight years.
- *And yet, men see physicians less often, take fewer days off from work, and spend less time convalescing in bed than women.* [3]

Once again, the masculine myth puts today's man in an anger-producing double bind. The rough-and-tumble, snips-and-snails lifestyle foisted on him by our culture has exposed him to a great degree of mental and emotional stress and physical risk. Yet his ingrained self-reliance and competitiveness prohibits him from admitting that he is weak or incapacitated in any way. So we have countless numbers of men who ignore the need for periodic physical examinations, go to work ill when they should stay home and recuperate, and scoff at medical attention for injury and illness until their wives drag them to the doctor's office or emergency room.

Men get angry when they are slowed by physical illness because it's unmanly to be sick, to take medicine, to tell someone about a suspicious lump or pain, or to use sick leave for recuperation. But in reality men are just as vulnerable to physical weakness and illness as women. Coming to terms with masculine anger for a man requires coming to terms with his physical limitations and weakness. Perpetual masculine strength is a myth.

Big Boys Don't Cry

A man's supposedly superior strength extends into the emotional realm as well. From his earliest years he was warned against being a sissy or a cry-baby. Boys are supposed to be tough. Boys can take it. Displays of emotion are for girls. "Your sister can hug and kiss Grandpa," they heard their tough, World War II fathers say, "but you're a man, so you just shake his hand."

One man came face to face with the fallacy of this myth when his best friend was diagnosed as having a brain tumor. "When I found out about Eric's condition," he reflected, "I was calm and collected on the outside. I kept my emotions well hidden. But inside I was falling apart. Suddenly, I was a kid again, helplessly watching my father battle for his life after surgery to remove his brain tumor. I knew Eric was in for a struggle. I wanted to give him a hug and tell him I loved him. But I had all my years as a tough, strong man working against me. If Eric had been a girl, I wouldn't have had a problem sharing my feelings with her. But since Eric was a man, everything inside me told me that it was inappropriate for me to express my affection to him.

"When I visited him in the hospital a few hours before his surgery, Eric was sleepy. I could have easily given him a hug and verbalized my love then. But instead, just like a man, I gave him a punch on the shoulder and mumbled some dumb line about getting well soon.

"Fortunately, Eric recovered fully from his operation. I was eventually able to tell him face to face that I loved him. But I had to grow up some before I could do it."

Emotions are not a sign of weakness as the masculine myth insists. Emotions are a natural, normal human expression. When a man denies or suppresses his emotions, they will work their way to the surface in other ways, often anger-driven.

Religion Is for Women

The cultural myth of masculine strength also brushes away the necessity for religion. "Real" men insist that religion is a crutch for children, women, lily-livered men, and old folks — people who are afraid to take life by the horns and roll with the punches.

But the notion that religion is basically a feminine phenomenon is a myth that is only pervasive in the Western culture. Patrick Arnold, assistant professor of Old Testament at the University of San Diego, illustrates:

> An imaginary trip around the world might quickly shatter that idea. Listen to Buddhist monks in Tibet as they shake their monastery with the deep-throated *aum*. Witness throngs of Hindu men making their annual pilgrimage to Benares. Watch a sea of Muslim males pray passionately to Allah in a huge Arabian mosque. Join Hasidic men in Jerusalem as they *doven* earnestly in prayer at the Western Wall. See the joyous faces of African tribesmen, scarred with ritual signs of their manhood. Pray with Mexican *penitentes* as they approach Guadalupe on their knees. Sweat in a South Dakota *initipi* ("life-lodge") as holy men fast and pray in the Lakota fashion. Or, for that matter, join charismatic evangelicals at a local businessmen's prayer breakfast. Everywhere around the world, at this moment, a billion men are seeking their God, fasting for visions, expiating their sins, singing divine praises and enduring hardships for faith and justice. Men are naturally deeply religious, all right; it is just that our modern culture provides little help for them anymore in finding their natural masculine spirituality.[4]

The tension between a man's need for a relationship with God and our culture's insistence that no such need exists is a cause of masculine anger.

Men Don't Need Friends Like Women Do

Our Nebraska farmer in chapter 2, Farrell Courtney, had a lot of good male friends. Men in that agrarian society counted on each other for everything. They helped each other build barns, harvest crops, rebound from natural disasters, and round up stray animals. Their success as a community depended on the mutual caring and support of the men.

Not so with Farrell's grandson, Bill, the Los Angeles machinist. He worked with a large factory full of men, many of whom he considered his friends because they swapped stories in the lunch room for 45 minutes each day. And he had his golf foursome and his Saturday night poker buddies. But these friends didn't enjoy a deep level of caring, transparency, support, or accountability. Bill didn't share his fears, his desires, his dreams, and his motivations with these men. "Men just don't do that kind of thing in the lunch room, on the golf course, or around a poker table," Bill might have said. "Liz might need a relationship like that with other women, because she's stuck at home alone all day. But I'm around men all the time. I don't need other friends."

Like Bill, today's man has been programmed to believe that relationships are the domain of women. Developing and maintaining transparent, nurturing friendship is often considered a feminine trait. Men look with suspicion at other men who have close male friends.

Yet in order to meet the basic psychological needs to know and be known, to love and be loved by others, men need deep caring relationships with other men. It's to this level that James instructed Christians, "Confess your sins to each other and pray for each other so that you may be healed" (James 5:16). A man who doesn't have at least one other man to whom he can be accountable regarding his failures, hurts, and temptations is a prime target for masculine anger.

The angry man in our society is caught between mythical masculinity on the one side and true masculinity on the other. He feels the pressure to achieve, to earn, to conquer, to win — and to do all these things on his own. But he also feels the need to love and to nurture those he loves, and to be loved and nurtured by those who love him. He futilely attempts to reconcile the two in his own life. He is torn between being invincible and vulnerable, aloof and involved, self-serving and succoring. As we shall see in the next chapter, the roots of this conflict send up numerous shoots of anger-producing tendencies in his life.

Think about It, Talk about It with Him

1. As a child, to what extent were you influenced by the cultural sex roles prescribing that girls are supposed to be soft and warm while boys are supposed to be rough and tumble?

Not	Mildly	Moderately	Strongly
influenced	influenced	influenced	influenced

2. What cultural difficulties do men and women face when they fail to live within their culturally prescribed sex roles?

3. To what extent do you think your man's behavior is dictated by the cultural myths of masculinity? Select a number for each myth (0 means "not at all affected," 10 means "totally affected," etc.). Then for each myth write a brief statement explaining the evidence that caused you to select the number you did:

I am what I do

0   1   2   3   4   5   6   7   8   9   10

I am what I earn

0   1   2   3   4   5   6   7   8   9   10

Real men always have great sex

0   1   2   3   4   5   6   7   8   9   10

Men must always be strong

0   1   2   3   4   5   6   7   8   9   10

Big boys don't cry

0   1   2   3   4   5   6   7   8   9   10

Religion is for women

0   1   2   3   4   5   6   7   8   9   10

Men don't need friends like women do

0   1   2   3   4   5   6   7   8   9   10

5. How would you evaluate your responses to your husband's frustration and anger about his sexual inadequacy? Respond to the following statements by circling the most appropriate word:

a. I encourage him to say no if he's not in the mood. I let him know I understand that he's a person, not a machine.

Always   Often   Sometimes   Seldom   Never

b. I often make the first advance in initiating sex, understanding that he likes to be appreciated and to have me participate enthusiastically.

Always   Often   Sometimes   Seldom   Never

c. I help him conquer any feelings of guilt he may have if I don't have an orgasm or if we don't experience orgasm together by assuring him that such happenings are normal.

Always   Often   Sometimes   Seldom   Never

d. I tell him how much I like him, how much I like his body, and how exciting I find his lovemaking.

Always   Often   Sometimes   Seldom   Never

e. If his erection subsides too soon, I assure him that it's nobody's fault and that lovemaking is far from over. I continue to express affection, realizing that lovemaking is more than just intercourse.

Always   Often   Sometimes   Seldom   Never

f. I discuss my sexual concerns with him out of bed — never during intercourse — when we are both feeling relaxed and secure in our relationship.

Always   Often   Sometimes   Seldom   Never [5]

3

Exposing the Roots of Mythical Masculinity

The myths of masculinity are flourishing in our culture because they have such a well-developed root system. If you hope to understand the anger in men caused by the unrealistic demands these myths place upon them, you will need to have some insight regarding their impetus and sustenance. In order to demythologize the myths of masculinity you must pull them out by the roots.

The Mama's Boy and the Playboy

Men learn how to be men from the example of their fathers and the instruction of their mothers. As illustrated by the Courtney family of the 1950s, Bobby's caricature of manhood came from his hardworking father who was too busy making his mark in the world to mentor his son. Like Bobby, many of today's men grew up spending most of their time with their mothers in the absence of their fathers. Observing their fathers from a distance, these sons, who are today's husbands and fathers, perceive that achieving a successful career, financial security, and a comfortable lifestyle are more important than the supposedly feminine tasks of nurturing relationships with children, friends, and God. Boys like Bobby become angry men in adulthood because their fathers have not prepared them for their role as men.

Mothers are often their husbands' unwitting accomplices in perpetuating these myths. They idolize their husbands in their sons' hearing by saying things like, "Your Daddy is such a good father. He works hard so we can have a big house and nice things. I hope you grow up to be just like Daddy." Indirectly a mother may influence her son to adopt the mythological masculine lifestyle by pressuring her husband to work longer hours, earn more money, and seek promotions in order to provide the luxuries she wants. Some mothers even groom their sons to be the tough, competent men in their lives that their husbands never were, because of their absence from the family.

If your man grew up in a home where the myths of masculinity were perpetrated in this way, it is important that he be exposed to alternative adult father and mother figures who reflect more positive parental roles.

Another prime purveyor of mythical masculinity is the media. It's hard to find a male character on television or in the movies who represents true masculinity. The myths of masculinity are strongly propagated throughout the entertainment industry.

One prominent caricature of masculinity in the media is the playboy. He's a bed-hopping adventurer with an insatiable sexual appetite. He can successfully maintain a number of sexual relationships simultaneously, and he never suffers the side effects of guilt, paternity suits, or disease. His women are always ready, willing, and able; they *never* have headaches when he comes to call.

Another mythical male running loose in the media is the tough guy. This is the iron-pumping, hard-driving, machismo-dripping Rambo type who doesn't take any guff from anybody. If his boss crosses him, he slugs him and quits. If his wife or kids hassle him, he's gone. In his disdain for the law, he makes all law enforcement agents look like the Keystone Cops. And he can blow away a bad guy without a thought for the grief he may bring to the poor man's loved ones. The tough guy does what he wants to do when he wants to do it, and nobody stands in his way.

A man trying to live up to these cartoon-like misrepresentations of masculinity will find himself frustrated and angry. The playboy/tough guy lifestyle looks so exciting. But he knows that if he dabbles in it, he could end up unemployed, divorced, or in trouble with the law.

But what are his alternatives? All the rest of the men in the media are spineless numbskulls continually being outsmarted by their wives, kids, and bosses. For decades Dagwood Bumstead has been a lovable albeit bumbling jerk, a pushover for Blondie, the kids, and his boss, Mr. Dithers. Even in the Huxtables, the model TV family of the '80s, Cliff ends up the goat much of the time, and Claire is never the goat. Furthermore, ministers and their male parishioners in the media are depicted as religious fanatics who are completely out of touch with the real world. Any male characters who reflect even a hint of moral or spiritual depth are portrayed not only as wimpy but wacko.

The antidote to the overpowering misrepresentation of masculinity in the media is to counterbalance the media's message in your man's life. Warmly and continuously affirm his adequacy as your sexual partner and the head of the family. Assure him that you're not looking for a muscle-bound, world-conquering, ladder-climbing tycoon, but for a caring friend and lover, a spiritual partner, and a nurturing father for your children.

Whenever possible, expose yourselves to positive models of masculinity in the media. For example, rent films like the

Oscar-winning *Chariots of Fire* and watch them together. Discuss together the courage and conviction of characters like Eric Liddell, the Scottish runner turned missionary. When you see positive qualities exhibited in a man on TV, say something like, "I really admire a man who values his family above his work." The more exposure to true masculinity you both can experience — without your mothering him or pestering him — the easier it will be for both of you to demystify masculinity.

Where Does the Anger Start?

The anger men feel today is rooted in the lack of a father/mentor and the pressure of mythical masculinity. Yet there are a number of secondary sources of masculine anger that spring from the two major sources we have already discussed. When one or more of these attitudes persists, it's just a matter of time before his anger goes off, probably in a manner that will be hurtful to him and those he loves.

Social Immaturity

Tom and Marge have three grown children who have launched into successful careers. During most of their married life Tom worked two jobs in order to finance the kids' college education. As a result, Tom didn't socialize much as the kids were growing up. He would often come home from work, eat supper in silence, and retire to the TV and his newspaper until bedtime. Tom and Marge rarely saw friends on the weekend because of Tom's part-time job Saturday and Sunday evenings. And on Thanksgiving or other social occasions with relatives or friends, Tom always came late and left early, claiming that he was too tired to visit.

A week after their last child left the nest and Tom quit his weekend job, Marge invited a small group from their adult Sunday school class for dinner. With the pressure finally off Tom, Marge thought that he would enjoy getting to know some people. But when she told him her plans, Tom was obviously upset. "I don't want any people over," he said at last. "I've worked hard all these years, and I deserve some peace and quiet."

Marge told him she was sorry, but that the invitations had already been sent out. During the dinner party Tom was distant and cool, speaking only when spoken to. After dinner, while everyone was bringing their plates into the kitchen, Tom slipped out the back door and didn't come back until after everyone had left. He continued to resist all of Marge's efforts to get him involved with people at church or in the neighborhood.

Men like Tom who are withdrawn, distant from others, lacking confidence in relationships, and excessively self-conscious may be holding back a tidal wave of anger. They usually have a great deal of insecurity and are easily slighted or injured by others. But they often tend to view the expression of feelings in interpersonal contexts as socially undesirable. They have not developed the social skills which would help them relieve the pressure of the anger inside. These men may appear controlled on the outside, but their anger is building up inside, looking for an escape valve.

Lack of Control

The macho masculine image is that of a man who is the captain of his own ship and the master of his fate. Most men want to be in complete control of all the elements of their lives. They want to be the unchallenged boss at home, and they want increasing measures of control over others at work. Many men break their backs to get to the top in their field or to own their own company because it fulfills the masculine dream of being top dog.

But few men actually achieve total control of their lives. And those who crave control in an area where they can't achieve it are often angry men. Is your man especially controlling in your relationship, such as demanding that he sign all the checks or handle all the money? Does he often criticize his boss, claiming, "I could do a much better job of running the company than that bozo"? Is he critical of others in authority over him: his father, the pastor, the government, the police officer who pulled him over for speeding? If so, he's probably dealing with an undercurrent of anger from a lack of control.

Unrealistic Expectations

Myron, age 30, runs one of the biggest restaurants in the downtown business district of a large city. "I used to be a raving lunatic at work," he confessed. "Every time I went into the kitchen I'd yell at the cooks because they were wasting too much food. I'd yell at the waitresses and the busboys for moving too slow. If my people didn't live up to my standards, which was most of the time, I'd jump all over them."

Myron finally realized that his outbursts at work were killing him, so he sought counseling. "I discovered that I was perpetually angry at work because I expected everyone to be perfect," Myron said. "It was the business my father had built. I felt responsible for keeping his high standards, but nobody could do it the way Dad could, and that made me angry."

If you looked in on Myron now at the restaurant you would find him joking and laughing with his staff. He enjoys coming to work because he realizes that nobody's perfect. Instead of yelling at his people, he uses that energy to teach them and encourage them, and they're responding by doing a better job.

Many men have difficulty accepting their limitations and the limitations of others. They can't accept their inability to accomplish something. They can't enjoy the status quo because it falls short of what they'd hoped for. And when they reach a goal, they are often disappointed because the material gains did not bring the satisfaction they expected. Failure to deal with unrealistic expectations will keep a furnace of anger burning hot inside.

Low Self-Worth

As soon as Darrell walked in the door his eight-year-old son, Luke, was on him. "Remember, Dad," Luke began excitedly as Darrell fumbled to hang his overcoat in the entry closet, "you said you would take me to the baseball card shop today."

"I don't think so, Luke," Darrell mumbled, his tone reflecting the unpleasant day that still weighed on him. "I'm not up to it, Son. Maybe we can go Saturday."

"But, Dad," Luke whined, "you promised to take me last Saturday, then Tuesday after school, and now today. I've saved my allowance for some cards I want. You have to take me today."

Darrell slammed the closet door angrily. "Luke, don't tell me what I have to do," he growled. "I'll take you to the card shop when I'm good and ready. Now, go to your room until your mother calls you for dinner." Darrell shoved Luke roughly in the direction of his bedroom.

Darrell's harsh response to Luke had been brewing for several weeks. His anger can be traced to his failing self-image due to numerous problems at work. Sales in Darrell's department have been declining for several weeks. As a result, he had to lay off one of his employees, who in turn criticized Darrell to his face as the cause of the decline. Other employees have been avoiding him at work, and today his boss bawled him out for not putting in enough hours trying to turn his department around. Darrell has extensive education and experience in his field. But from all the negative input he is receiving, he has the gnawing feeling that he can't cut it in the arena where men must succeed: his career.

Men like Darrell with a low sense of self-worth are often reservoirs of unresolved anger. A man's low self-image is usually the result of threats of an interpersonal nature, such as insults or undue criticism. Studies show that men with a high sense of self-worth are much less affected by criticism.

Insults and criticism are especially provocative of anger if the man already suffers from self-esteem instability relating to poor social adjustment, depression, anxiety, and low life satisfaction. These men usually did not receive the affirmation they craved from their fathers during childhood, and they get angry when they are not affirmed and appreciated as adults. No matter how hard he tries, the man with low self-worth never quite measures up to the idealized vision of what others expect him to be. He may appear to be quite confident and secure, but in reality he is insecure and highly sensitive to the criticism of others, positive or negative.

A man's anger in response to his low self-worth serves a number of functions. It prompts him to express his displeasure at the affront he has suffered. It helps him defend himself against all his negative feelings. It encourages him to restore his wounded self-esteem and public self-image by going on the offensive. Yet in the process of trying to save his own skin, he may bring pain to others, especially those closest to him.

Incompetence

Another source of masculine anger is a man's sense that he is ill-equipped or unable to do what is expected of him. Much of this anger comes from his failure to live up to the cultural masculine imperatives: strength, success, financial security, sexual prowess, etc.

A man may be angry because he will never be as strong as his father or successful enough to earn his mother's approval. He may have set unrealistic goals for himself that he cannot attain. For example, he may have determined to be president of the company by age 35 and retired by age 45, only to realize that he is locked into a middle management position because he just doesn't have the abilities to meet his own goals. Or he may be angry simply because he can no longer keep up with the young bucks on the racquetball court.

Many men feel stress and frustration due to their incompetence in situations that require "feminine" behaviors. A good example is the man mentioned in the last chapter whose friend was facing brain surgery. The man's inability to support his friend in a tender, nurturing way (which is perceived by most men as a feminine trait) caused him great turmoil. Many men experience a similar frustration when their wives want them to be more affectionate, talk about their feelings, or take the initiative in relationships with their friends. Feelings of incompetence in areas that are traditionally feminine often translate into expressions of anger.

Guilt

Jeff's only complaint in his three-year marriage to Dana was that she didn't want to have sex as often as he did. One Saturday morning he woke up feeling especially amorous. He tried to arouse Dana sexually, but she resisted because "fooling around" would make her late for her brunch date with a college girlfriend. Jeff persisted playfully until Dana struggled to free herself from his grasp and get out of bed. Then he overpowered her and forced himself on her.

In the four months since that morning, Dana and Jeff haven't slept together. At first she moved out to the couch. But when she was ready to move back into the bedroom several days later, Jeff lashed out at her angrily, blaming her for the incident. He knows that he hurt her deeply, and he feels terribly guilty about it. But his pride won't let him admit to himself or confess to Dana that he did in fact rape her. He doesn't think he can ever forgive himself. The angry tension between his guilt and pride is driving him and Dana farther apart.

Men have difficulty forgiving themselves for the mistakes they make. It's all part of the masculine myth of strength and superiority that considers admission of wrong an unthinkable weakness. They cannot escape the guilt they feel for hurting their wives, children, or coworkers. But their masculine pride prevents them from confessing it, apologizing for it, and seeking forgiveness from those they've offended. And since it's unmanly to admit to guilt, the emotional pressure is vented in the form of anger, often toward the very party from whom he should seek forgiveness.

Fear

Growing up under such a great cloud of cultural expectations for masculinity breeds fear in many men. They are afraid of not measuring up to parental expectations, career requirements, or personal goals. They are afraid that others will be in control of their lives. They are afraid of failing in their work, in their marriages, in their sexual function, and in their faith. They are afraid of dying, and they are afraid that they won't be missed once they're gone.

As with guilt, fear is something men don't want to admit. Men are supposed to be brave, fearless warriors. Many men are unable to admit and deal with their fear, so it is translated into anger and appears as a fight response.

Failure

Men tend to react in anger when confronted by failure. They have difficulty forgiving themselves for mistakes, cutting their losses, and moving ahead. Instead they are often obsessed with lists of "if only's": If only I had spent more time with the client, I may have been able to save the account; if only I had gone into my father's business instead of striking out on my own, I would be financially secure by now; if only I had been more consistent about spending time with my son, he probably wouldn't be in trouble today; if only I had purchased AT&T stock when it was lower, I could have made a killing.

Men often sense failure most keenly in their lovemaking. Much of a man's identity is wrapped up in his sexual performance. If he ejaculates too soon or can't bring his wife to orgasm, his culturally skewed value as a man is seriously tainted in his mind. She may say, "It's okay, Honey. It's not important. I still love you." But he has trouble hearing the "I love you" part, because his sexual performance is *very* important to him. For many men, failing at lovemaking is tantamount to failing at life. Many suicides and murder-suicides have resulted from a man's sense of failure in the sexual arena.

Men who cannot let go of their failures are angry men because they're wrestling with a past they cannot change. And by constantly affirming their past failures they end up prophesying and fulfilling failure in the future.

Role Confusion

Ron R. Lee aptly summarizes the role revolution in America and the frustration it has sparked in many men:

> In generations past, spouses found security in established roles. Men toiled for the daily bread; women baked it and served it to the family. But during the past quarter-century, all the rules have changed. More women have entered the work force, and they are taking advantage of new opportunities in the fields of business, finance, politics, even the military. For every Alan Alda who salutes today's "new women," there are a host of ordinary Joes who are bewildered, and sometimes threatened, by women who demand to be treated as equals in the work place as well as at home.[1]

Many men are angry today because the women in their lives aren't as predictable as they were a generation ago. Increasing numbers of the women they work with have ascended from secretary, data entry, and assembler positions to compete with them for managerial positions and junior partnerships.

What's more, his wife doesn't seem to be fulfilled in the traditional role of washing, cleaning, cooking, and changing diapers. She wants a better education. She wants a shot at a career. She wants to begin a home business in her spare time. Men are asking, "Am I the bread-winner in the family or not? *And if I'm not, what am I?*"

The revolution has even reached the inner sanctum of masculine domain—the bedroom. With the feminist movement has come volumes of material on female sexuality. Today's woman is better informed about her and her husband's sexual needs and more aggressive about seeing that those needs are met. Many men are uncomfortable or ambivalent about their wives' new sexual assertiveness. A man's culturally ingrained expectation that he must lead during sex may leave him feeling out of control and insecure when his wife takes the initiative in sex.

The man who was raised on the myths of masculinity may be threatened and confused by the revolution in sex roles. And unwilling as he is to allow his fear and insecurity to be known, he reacts in anger in the areas he cannot control.

Losses

Being culturally conditioned to hit it big and win in every arena, men often have difficulty dealing with losses in their lives. Winning is everything. Losing is for losers. Real men don't lose often, and when they do they go down fighting. As in other areas of life they are unable to control, men often react to loss in anger.

When Roger's father died, Roger didn't cry, and he didn't say much to anyone about how he felt. Like most men, Roger wasn't very experienced in verbalizing what was going on inside him. But after the funeral he stayed at the cemetery alone and beat his fist against the headstone until his hand bled. Roger's angry reaction to the loss of his father is repeated in many men who lose family members and friends to death.

The inability to handle losses keeps a man caught in the anger stage of grieving and also ignites anger in other forms. Men who lose valuable time on a work project, who lose their businesses to bankruptcy, or who lose money in the stock market may find themselves lashing out at others or searing themselves inside with the anger of unresolved grief.

The anger that men experience from these many sources does not simply evaporate into thin air like rain after a storm. Rather, unresolved anger builds up like steam in a boiler. Eventually that anger will explode, sometimes in ways that are harmful to the angry man and others around him. In the next chapter we will explore a number of the ways masculine anger is expressed.

Think about It, Talk about It with Him

1. Is your husband influenced by the media to copy the "playboy" or "tough guy" image of cultural masculinity? If so, in what way?

The playboy image

Not influenced	Mildly influenced	Moderately influenced	Strongly influenced

The tough guy image

Not influenced	Mildly influenced	Moderately influenced	Strongly influenced

2. To what extent have any of the following attitudes been a problem in your man's understanding and expression of true masculinity?

Social immaturity

No problem	Small problem	Moderate problem	Great problem

Lack of control

No problem	Small problem	Moderate problem	Great problem

Unrealistic expectations

No problem	Small problem	Moderate problem	Great problem

Low self-worth

No problem	Small problem	Moderate problem	Great problem

Incompetence

No problem	Small problem	Moderate problem	Great problem

Guilt

No problem	Small problem	Moderate problem	Great problem

Fear

No problem	Small problem	Moderate problem	Great problem

Failure

No problem	Small problem	Moderate problem	Great problem

Role confusion

No problem	Small problem	Moderate problem	Great problem

Losses

No problem	Small problem	Moderate problem	Great problem

4

Anger Out of Bounds

Is it wrong for a man (or a woman for that matter) to be angry? Definitely not. Anger is a natural human response, a facet of the emotional warning system that God built into our bodies to alert us to problems and prompt us to positive problem-solving actions. Even Jesus experienced anger, as most clearly evidenced in biblical literature when He drove the moneychangers out of the Temple.

But anger becomes problematic instead of problem-solving when it boils over the boundaries. What are the boundaries for anger? When does a man's anger go out of bounds and become a threat to him and others in his life?

Rebellion without a Cause

Remember Cliff, the fearless killer of stubborn lawn mowers? When he mortally wounded his Lawn Boy with a deer rifle, the mower wasn't the real cause of his anger. The machine's inability to perform might have been the match that lit the fuse. But the bundle of emotional dynamite that it touched off had been in place for a long time. When Janice finally got Cliff to talk about the incident, he admitted that he had been upset for some time because he wasn't receiving the attention from her he wanted. He also confessed that he was disappointed with his children for not living up to his expectations.

But why was he really angry at Janice and the kids? Where did his unmet expectations come from? What was the tap root of his anger? At that point Cliff didn't know and neither did Janice. They didn't realize the impact that Cliff's strained relationship with his father had on his emotions and behavior. They weren't aware how much the myths of masculinity were affecting his self-image. It was only after the couple began meeting with a counselor that the real roots of his anger came to light and were dealt with.

Men who are angry without knowing why almost always express it in ways that are unhealthy and destructive to themselves and others. This type of anger is called *free-floating* anger, because the victim is on the brink of anger or actually angry much of the time without an obvious cause. It's also called *impotent* anger, because, even in an apparent show of power, the victim is powerless to deal with his anger because he can't identify its cause.

This isn't the kind of anger we see in Jesus as He cleared the Temple. His anger was neither free-floating nor impotent; it rose with a specific stimulus and receded with an appropriate response. Jesus knew exactly what drove His anger. He said, "Is it not written: 'My house will be called a house of prayer for all nations'? But you have made it 'a den of robbers'" (Mark 11:17). His response to His anger was in bounds because it was measured precisely to alleviate the problem.

Impotent, free-floating anger tends to build up in men. They don't know what's behind it, so they don't know how to vent it. So it accumulates and grows within them like boiling magma in the heart of a dormant volcano. The anger is there, buried deep within. It's boiling. Sooner or later something will trigger it, and it will go off in a hurtful way.

But you never know when or where a man's anger will explode, because *he* doesn't know when or where it will explode. German psychologist Karl Bednarik vividly describes the problem:

> This anger is inarticulate because it does not even know what it wants. Rarely does it reach the point of action, and when it does, the action seems to be other than intended. A rebellion "without a cause" directs itself at random targets, comes to light in mysterious acts of violence, outbursts of blind rage, incoherent criticism, aimless resentment, dreary grumbling, or else in apathetic, helpless, sulky resignation. . . . And this explosion usually — in fact, nearly always — involves innocent people: subordinates, our own wives and children, individuals who happen to cross our path.[1]

You Can't Do That to Me!

Much of human anger is out of bounds because it springs from selfishness. A man may get angry at his father for not including him in the business, at his wife for not serving the dinner he expected, at his daughter for telephoning at midnight for a ride home from a party, or at his son for not weeding the garden when he wanted it done. He may explode with rage at a driver who cuts him off on the freeway, at a long red light that makes him late for an appointment, or at a television that gives up the ghost in the middle of the big game. In his classic book, *Caring Enough to Confront*, David Augsburger describes this self-centered anger as "a demand that also demands others meet your demands."[2] In short, self-centered anger erupts when you don't get what you want when you want it. This kind of anger is out of bounds.

Self-centered anger is not what Jesus experienced and expressed in the Bible. He wasn't ticked at the moneychangers for offending Him but for desecrating His Father's house and disrupting the worship of the people. Jesus never got angry at the wrongs done to Him—including the ultimate wrong, the crucifixion. Instead He forgave. But He did get angry whenever someone cast a slur on His Father or treated others unjustly.

In order to defuse a man's anger, he needs to examine his motives to see if they are springing from self-centeredness or God-centeredness.

No "Second-Day Anger"

By definition, anger is a temporary emotional arousal that occurs, is handled, and recedes in a matter of minutes or, at the most, a few hours. Anger that is allowed to fester and seethe for days, weeks, or months is out of bounds. Notice that the angry Jesus dealt with the situation in the Temple, and then His anger dissipated. We don't see Him stomping off to Bethany kicking dogs along the road or snarling at His disciples. Once the Temple incident was handled, it was over. He came back to the Temple in a few days to teach, and nothing more was said about the confrontation.

Paul instructed: "Do not let the sun go down while you are still angry" (Ephesians 4:26). Author and pastor Calvin Miller calls anger that's held overnight "second-day anger." He writes, "This tendency to nurse our anger overnight always builds to a grudge, which eats at the soul and finally rots it with cynicism. Over time, a grudge becomes poisonous bitterness." [3]

Second-day anger is out of bounds. Unresolved anger accrues increased explosiveness the way an unpaid loan accrues snowballing interest. Today's anger must be dealt with today, or it will be even more difficult to deal with tomorrow.

The main reason men don't deal with their anger sooner, as mentioned earlier in the chapter, is that they don't know what they're really angry about. They can't deal with their anger because they don't know what they are dealing with. As we have seen, the roots of most masculine anger are buried deep in the process of how a boy grows to be a man in our culture. A man can shoot his lawn mower, fight with his father, have an affair, or kill his wife believing that he is finally venting his anger. But until he discovers its cultural and/or psychological roots, his anger will compound day after day only to explode again in a non-productive way.

No Hostility and No Aggression

Anger is also out of bounds when it escalates to hostility or aggression. What's the difference? When a man is angry at his wife, child, parents, boss, coworker, customer, etc., he experiences a momentary feeling of displeasure toward that person. Ideally the feeling of anger alerts him to a problem in the relationship that he moves to resolve immediately. Anger handled this way is well within bounds.

However, if he fails to deal with his anger, it may grow into hostility: the desire to hurt, to punish, or to gain vengeance on the person who prompts the displeasure. And unresolved hostility can lead to aggression: intended or actual harm committed. The harmful deeds provoked by hostility and aggression are the painful dividends paid by held-over anger.

There is no evidence in the Bible to suggest that Jesus had any intention of harming the moneychangers or the animal handlers. He knocked over the money tables, but he didn't knock down the people who manned them. He used a small whip of cords to drive the animals out of the Temple, but He didn't strike their handlers. His anger was focused, controlled, in bounds.

Why has domestic violence become such a widespread problem in our culture? Largely because deep-seated masculine anger has fermented to the boiling point and spilled over into hostility and aggression. Sexual molestation, abuse, rape, hatred, muggings, beatings, murder, gang violence, freeway shootings, suicide—all are evidence of anger out of bounds.

Even when anger explodes in "socially acceptable" ways (e.g., a customer cussing out a clerk for bad service, an employer verbally reaming out a gold-bricking employee, a husband belittling his wife in front of their friends), more harm than good is done. Augsburger writes, "Explosive anger is powerless to effect change in relationships. It dissipates needed energies, stimulates increased negative feelings, irritates the other persons in the transaction and offers nothing but momentary discharge. Vented anger may ventilate feelings and provide instant though temporary release for tortured emotions, but it does little for relationships." [4]

Underground Anger

A lot of people, especially Christians, have a problem with Jesus being angry. They may call His outburst in the Temple "righteous indignation," but they won't admit that he was angry because "everybody knows that anger is a sin."

This mentality has caused many men to push their anger out of bounds in another direction—denying it, suppressing it, or pretending it isn't there, because to them it's wrong to be angry. As we shall see in the next chapter, suppressed anger is just as harmful to an angry man as explosive hostility and aggression is to those around an angry man.

Jesus didn't suppress his anger any more than He exploded with rage that day in the Temple. His anger was up front, out in the open. He responded to the situation quickly, positively, and appropriately, then went on with His business.

If a man buries his anger inside, he's only storing up pressure for a later implosion (hurting himself) and/or explosion (hurting others). If he doesn't bring his anger to the surface and deal with it, someday, somewhere, somehow it will express itself in an out-of-bounds manner, and somebody will get hurt—and that somebody may be you. In the next chapter we will take a close look at the various ways masculine anger boils to the surface.

Think about It, Talk about It with Him

1. What evidence do you see, if any, that your husband is influenced by *impotent, free-floating anger?* Why is his impotent, free-floating anger such a potential danger to you?

2. What evidence do you see, if any, that your husband is influenced by *self-centered anger?* Why is his self-centered anger such a potential danger to you?

3. What evidence do you see, if any, that your husband is influenced by *second-day anger?* Why is his second-day anger such a potential danger to you?

4. What evidence do you see, if any, that your husband is influenced by his anger to commit *hostility and aggression?* Why is his hostility and aggression such a potential danger to you?

5. What evidence do you see, if any, that your husband is influenced by *underground anger?* Why is his underground anger such a potential danger to you?

5

When Anger Boils
to the Surface

Imagine that four men — call them Frank, Joe, Karl, and Stan — work for the same large manufacturing plant. They are typical of their gender in that success in their careers is of high value to each of them. Any threat to their job, financial security, or career advancement is a source of frustration, irritation, and anger. Lately, the company has not been doing well, and each man fears being laid off.

One day, Mr. Bernard, the president of the company, addresses all his employees over the plant public address system: "I'm sorry to inform you that our company has suffered heavy, irretrievable financial losses. In 30 days the plant will close, and you will all be unemployed. I wish you all the best of luck in your next job."

Frank, who is known around the plant for his low boiling point, instantly explodes. "You can't do this to me, Bernard!" he bellows as he bursts out of his office and heads toward the president's office. "You're not getting away with this, not after all I've done for this company, all the hours I've put in, and all the blood I've sweat!" Frank brusquely pushes aside several wide-eyed coworkers as he rumbles down the hall.

Reaching the executive complex, Frank barges into the outer office with such force that the glass in the door shatters. Ignoring the secretary's warning to stop, he bursts into Mr. Bernard's office just as the president is reaching for the phone to call security. Frank blasts his boss with every expletive in the book as Mr. Bernard shuffles to keep the desk between him and his livid employee. Within moments two security guards rush in and restrain Frank, who refuses to leave the office without a struggle.

Meanwhile, Joe listens to Mr. Bernard's announcement while pacing around his desk. His face is contorted in anguish, and he can't keep from wringing his hands nervously. "You're a jerk, Bernard," Joe mutters under his breath. Then, after glancing around to make sure no one is watching, he reaches into the bottom drawer of his desk and pulls out a half-full pint of vodka. He slides the bottle discreetly into a stack of papers and carries it deep into the meandering canyon of file cabinets at the end of his floor.

Making sure no one can see him, Joe takes a gulp from the bottle and grimaces as he swallows the fiery liquid. In the day-to-day pressures Joe faces at work, usually one good swig from the bottle is enough. But not today. He replays Mr. Bernard's announcement in his mind repeatedly, concluding each replay with another swallow. Soon the bottle is empty and the filing cabinets begin to sway in his vision.

In another section of the plant, Karl receives Mr. Bernard's announcement while sitting at his bench repairing components. If you were to judge Karl's level of concern by his physical or vocal response, you might believe that he didn't even hear the announcement. His posture is unchanged. His hand-held tools keep moving deftly over the component. The only clue that Karl is affected by the announcement is the barely noticeable clenching of his jaw.

A friend from a nearby department walks up to Karl and exclaims, "We may have to move out of state to find another job like this! We may be out of work for months! What are we going to do?" Karl turns his head slightly toward his coworker, then turns back to his bench, saying nothing. The man tries again to get Karl's opinion about the situation, but Karl is in another world. Frustrated, Karl's friend walks away.

Karl continues to work as if nothing has happened. But inside Karl's anger is boiling. He's not aware of it, but his blood pressure, respiration, and the acidity level in his stomach have all risen drastically. He can feel a major-league headache coming on, but he's not about to give the company the satisfaction of seeing him explode. So he bites his lip and keeps working.

Stan is just as upset about losing his job as are Frank, Joe, and Karl. After a few seconds of mild panic and frantic questioning, Stan picks up the phone and calls his wife at her office. "I've just heard some rather disturbing news," he begins. "The plant is going under. I'll be out of a job in a month."

"I'm sorry to hear that, Stan. How are you feeling right now?"

"I'm scared. It may take weeks or months to find another job. But I guess I'm more angry than anything else. For months I've been trying to suggest some cost-saving measures in our department, and nobody seemed to care. I'm angry at the executives for not being more cautious about costs. And I'm angry at myself for not doing a better job."

"Do you think the company might have survived if you had worked harder or longer?"

"Probably not. But it's so easy for me to get mad when I can't control the outcome."

"I know we'll handle it, Stan. Let's talk about it some more tonight at home."

"Thanks, Honey. I feel a little better already just getting it off my chest."

The Many Faces of Anger

This simple, fictional version of "The Day the Company Went Belly-Up" is designed to illustrate in general terms the primary ways by which masculine anger is expressed. Hot-headed Frank represents men whose anger explodes as outward hostility or rage. Vodka-swigging Joe represents men who displace their anger, expressing it in some form of compulsive/addictive behavior. Tight-lipped Karl represents men who suppress and internalize their anger. And Stan represents men who have learned — often with the help and encouragement of their wives — to acknowledge and verbalize their anger in a positive and productive way. Of course, no man is exclusively a Frank, Joe, Karl, or Stan with respect to anger expression. Rather, men tend to sample from all four styles even when one dominates.

If we asked 1,000 men on the street which of these four ways is the right way to handle anger, we'd probably get at least 100 to 200 votes in each category. Some men like Frank would say, "You've got to blow off steam by kicking something, breaking something, or telling someone off. It's not healthy to hold it inside." Joe's supporters might say, "Having a couple of drinks is better than punching out your boss or slapping your wife or kids around." Those who side with Karl would argue, "Real men can master their anger just by clamping a lid on it." And Stan's fans, who would probably be in the minority because of his "unmasculine" approach, would insist, "Directing anger outward in a healthy, nonviolent way is the only way to keep anger from hurting or destroying you and your family."

If your man is more like Stan than Frank, Joe, or Karl, consider yourself blessed. A man who has learned to express his anger in positive ways is least likely to hurt himself, you, or your children. But the odds favor that you are more likely to be involved with a man who leans toward being a hot-head, an addict, or a strong, quiet macho-man with respect to his anger. This chapter will help you understand the potential danger you are in if a man fails to learn to deal with his anger according to Stan's example.

When Anger Leads to Rage

Calvin Miller capsulizes the description of masculine anger that explodes in rage, as illustrated by Frank in our story:

> Anger without focus is . . . a tantrum. Children often experience this unfocused anger, and they sometimes respond by flailing out with arms and legs, pounding the floor or whatever's handy, often screaming at an appropriate pitch. . . . Adults have their own variations of tantrums, such as the slugfest I witnessed recently in an overheated traffic jam—just plain rage.
> Tantrum anger indulges an immature response without regard for its source or effects.[1]

A man's hostile, outrageous expression of anger can take many forms and lead to a number of negative consequences for him and for you.

Poisoned Relationships

Men who allow their anger to explode in rage often poison their relationships in the process. A man in tantrum will often blast his wife, children, boss, or friends with thoughtless, hurtful words. He may slam the door in someone's face or abruptly hang up in the middle of a telephone conversation. And even if he later says, "I'm sorry, I lost my head; I didn't mean what I said," the damage has been done. The offended individual may graciously forgive him for his actions, but such offenses are not easily forgotten, especially when they recur—as they often do with explosive men.

Men who fly off the handle in anger poison their work relationships. It's likely that Frank, the hot-head in our story, and Mr. Bernard, his boss, didn't part company on the best of terms. Rather, it's easy to imagine that Frank didn't have to wait 30 days to start pounding the pavement. He was probably fired immediately and expelled from the plant for his vitriolic outburst in the president's office. Angry men like Frank also alienate themselves from their coworkers. Nobody likes to be around someone who may bite his head off at the drop of a hat.

If a man expresses his anger in an explosive fashion, he will have problems in his career. He probably will not be well liked by superiors, peers, or subordinates. He will likely be passed over for promotions. And he may be only one outburst away from receiving his walking papers. His anger is cutting him off from people at work. But it may also hurt you and your children if he loses his source of income because of it.

Men who explode in verbal rage also poison their relationships at home. They are often just as caustic toward their families as they are toward their bosses when things don't go the way they want. Frank could easily have gone home after his horrible day at the plant and continued to boil by criticizing or ridiculing his wife. Perhaps you still carry the emotional scars from hurtful words your man uttered in a fit of rage. If his improper expression of anger is not redirected, his poisonous words may eventually kill his relationship with you and your children.

Physical and Sexual Violence

Men like Frank are not only capable of crashing through office doors and bashing people with their words. They have been known to physically and sexually assault others in their rage, including their bosses, wives, girlfriends, and children. It's not unthinkable to imagine Frank wriggling free of the security guards in hopes of punching Mr. Bernard's lights out. More seriously, these are the kinds of men who return to their former jobs with a gun to open fire on anyone they see. Or they may become the next freeway, campus, or shopping mall sniper you hear about on the evening news.

Of even greater concern to you and your children, these men are often the perpetrators of physical and sexual violence on their loved ones. It's no coincidence that the phenomenon of masculine anger and incidents of physical and sexual violence they commit at home are escalating concurrently in our culture. Add to this formula the wide acceptance of sex and violence in today's movies, television, and music and you have a growing circle of men who take out their anger by raping, battering, or murdering their women and children.

How badly is the problem escalating? In June 1990, the Senate Judiciary Committee reported:

> • The rape rate is increasing four times as fast as the overall crime rate.
> • One in five adult women has been raped, one in six by someone she knows.
> • Between 3 million and 4 million women are beaten each year, 1 million so severely that they seek medical help.
> • More than half of all homeless women are fleeing domestic violence.[2]

Angry husbands and boyfriends are also attempting to kill their wives, girlfriends, and ex-girlfriends in increasing numbers, and some of them are succeeding. For example, during an eight-month period in 1989, Orange County, California, was the scene of the following reported incidents of husband/boyfriend perpetrated criminal violence:

> • A man shoots his ex-girlfriend a week after a judge ordered him to stay away from her. Then he shoots himself twice. Both are taken to the hospital in critical condition.
> • A man breaks bottles and dishes in the apartment of his former girlfriend and deliberately wounds himself. Then he holds police at bay for four hours.
> • A man shoots his former girlfriend then kills himself.
> • A man shoots and kills the son of his former girlfriend.

- A man kills his ex-girlfriend.
- A man shoots and kills his estranged wife.
- A man shoots and kills his former girlfriend and her male friend.
- A man kills his girlfriend.
- A man kills his estranged wife.[3]

For every reported act of rape, attempted rape, assault, and murder, there are thousands of unreported cases of domestic violence: wife battering, marital rape, and child abuse. If a man does not learn to deal with his anger positively, it may go off in the form of an explosion of rage that could physically hurt his wife, his child, or someone else.

When Anger Leads to Addiction

Instead of reaching for Mr. Bernard's throat as Frank did, Joe expressed his anger by reaching for a bottle. Joe knew that roughing up his boss verbally or physically wouldn't be very smart. His coworkers and his family might think less of him. He might damage his chances of getting a letter of recommendation from Mr. Bernard. And if he lost control and actually punched his boss, he may lose his last paycheck or get arrested.

Angry men like Joe are aware that hostile outbursts are embarrassing, self-defeating, and socially unacceptable. So they look for a more "suitable" way of relieving the pressure of their anger. Often the outlet they choose is more acceptable socially and less incriminating personally. But if these behaviors are only temporarily effective in dealing with anger, they will need to be repeated. The result may be compulsive/addictive behaviors that are ultimately as harmful to the angry man and his family as acts of rage.

Substance Addiction

Joe's pattern of dealing with his anger was to drown it in alcohol for a couple of hours. But for men like Joe, alcohol merely diffuses the anger and postpones the urgency of dealing with it. Other men seek the same release through the abuse of tobacco, over-the-counter and illegal drugs, and food. Since substance abuse doesn't really solve the problem, the repeated applications of these substances generate harmful and sometimes lethal addictions. Consider the following facts:

• Men tend to drink alcohol more to excess than women by a ratio of about 4:1. Men die at a greater rate than women from both natural and external causes of death which are associated with excessive drinking.
• Excessive alcohol consumption among men has been implicated as a factor contributing to the increased incidence of automobile fatalities and other accidental deaths among men. Alcohol is known to impair judgment and problem-solving ability and to decrease impulse control.
• Men who abuse alcohol are also at an increased risk of committing suicide and homicide, since alcohol tends to impair one's insight and ability to control impulsive, destructive, and self-destructive behavior.
• Men smoke at a significantly higher rate than women. They start smoking earlier, smoke more of each cigarette, inhale more deeply and more often, and smoke in a greater variety of forms than women. Smoking predisposes individuals to coronary artery disease, chronic bronchitis, emphysema, asthma, respiratory infection, and malignant neoplasms of the mouth, pharynx, respiratory system, ureter, and bladder.[4]

Another "substance" often abused by angry men is money. A man may try to diffuse his anger by buying things that help him prop up his failing image. He may make highly speculative and irresponsible investments in a frantic attempt to hit it big financially and get on top. He may become a compulsive gambler, pouring huge sums of money into the lottery or frequenting legal or illegal gambling establishments.

Substance abuse will eventually lead to trouble for the angry man and his family. Abuse of alcohol, tobacco, drugs, and food will impair his health and shorten his life. His addictions may also get him in trouble with the law: arrested for drunk driving, drug possession, illegal gambling, etc. Furthermore, a man's drinking, smoking, using, or spending habits will hurt you and your children through his physical or mental disability, early death, loss of income and/or savings, or arrest. If a man fails to deal properly with his anger, he may open the door to disaster in his family.

Sexual Addiction

Some men displace their anger through various forms of sexual addiction. A man may become addicted to pornographic magazines or films in order to perpetuate the intoxication of sexual arousal. He may try to soothe his rage and bolster his manhood by divorcing his wife or having an affair with someone younger, prettier, or sexier.

A man's unchallenged anger-driven sexual addiction will end up hurting the ones he loves. No matter how devoted you are, if he cannot find peace with himself he will eventually leave you physically or emotionally for another sexual partner or fantasy.

Religious Addiction

Byron was one of the most respected men in his church. He chaired the church board and sat on most other committees. He taught Sunday school, served as a greeter and usher, and was always the first to arrive and last to leave on church work days. Outside his local church, Byron was active in supporting international missions and the local Salvation Army post with his finances and volunteer service.

Seeing Byron as a devoted Christian and active church-man, his fellow parishioners were shocked when they heard about his nervous breakdown. If anyone were at peace with God and with himself, they thought, it was Byron. Yet most of Byron's zealous Christianity sprang from his desire to compensate for the anger that seemed to eat at him constantly. He felt that if he just got more involved in Christian activities, somehow God would overlook his "character flaw." Byron was, in effect, a religious fanatic. He understood that salvation was by grace through faith, but he wasn't sure that his day-to-day anger was completely covered. So he immersed himself in religious activity in an effort to earn God's approval. His frantic attempts to please God with activity didn't satisfy him. So he got more deeply involved until he burned himself out.

Men like Byron try to displace their anger by becoming religious zealots. This man interprets his anger as an evil he can somehow purge through excessive religious activity. The family of this man can be hurt as he increasingly abandons them in the name of ministry and service. The zealot is particularly difficult to dissuade from his fanaticism, because he believes he is doing God's work.

When Anger Goes Underground

In our opening story, Karl is pictured as a man of steel when it comes to expressing anger. Men like Karl feel that an outburst of rage like Frank's is unmanly because it reveals a lack of control. Furthermore, men of steel can master their vices, believing that expressing anger through some form of compulsive behavior is also a pitiful display of lack of control. Men like Karl pride themselves in keeping their emotions wrapped securely inside.

When a man tries to deal with his anger by burying it inside, it's like trying to deal with a live grenade by hiding it under his coat. He may talk himself into believing that suppressed anger just goes away. And he may be able to fool himself and others for a period of time. But eventually the grenade is going to explode, and he and everybody around him will be painfully aware how wrong he was. Suppressed anger doesn't go away. It simmers, then boils, and finally implodes, often devastating the man and his family.

One of the first signs that a man is suppressing his anger is a tendency to withdraw and isolate himself from people. There are a couple of reasons why he may do this.

First, he's trying very hard to hold everything inside and maintain a serene, "everything's okay" exterior. That's hard work. He may easily get depressed in the process, prompting him to want to run away and hide.

Second, since hassles with people are often the cause of the anger he must work so hard to suppress, he may unconsciously begin to shun people and social situations in order to avoid provocation to anger. After all, if he sidesteps anger-producing situations, he has less anger to hide.

Unfortunately, since family tensions often provoke anger, this man may even withdraw from his wife and children. He leaves for work early and returns home late. When he's home, he buries himself in the newspaper or television, retreats to his den or shop, or escapes to the golf course or his favorite fishing hole alone. Dialogue with this man is strictly at a surface level. For all practical purposes, his wife is a widow and his children are fatherless.

Being Eaten Alive

Men who fail to deal with their anger properly, either by burying it under a steel exterior, exploding in rage, or displacing it through compulsive/addictive behaviors, will pay a high physical price. More and more experts agree that anger and hostility can be hazardous to a man's health, particularly his heart.

Ben, 52, is the publisher of a small-town newspaper who has channeled his anger and hostility into his work. The great volume and frantic pace of his work used to keep him running at high speed day and night. "I had a hard time staying up with the work," Ben admits. "I'd come home late every night with a pizza in one hand and a stack of work in the other. I even got a lap board so I could work while sitting on the 'john.' I figured I'd save time and get more done if I could do four things at once."

Ben's driven lifestyle included angry eruptions at people who got in his way. He often snapped at his wife and kids for bothering him while he worked at home. He was curt and demanding with his employees. Anybody who didn't jump to his tune would be the target of his blistering reprimand or cold shoulder.

But Ben's hostile approach to life eventually took its toll. Just after returning from a publishers' convention, he felt the classic pains in his shoulder, arms, and neck. In the emergency room at 3 A.M. a heart attack was diagnosed. Luckily, Ben survived. But half a million Americans each year don't.

Dr. Redford Williams, professor of psychiatry at Duke University Medical Center, says that hostility has three stages, and he gives this example:

You are on an express line at the supermarket where the sign says, "No more than 10 items."

Stage One: Distrust of others. You count the items in the baskets of people in front of you. You *expect* somebody to cheat and thereby take advantage of you.

Stage Two: You *feel* angry when you find somebody cheating. The guy in front of you has 12 items.

Stage Three: You *show* the anger by saying something nasty to the "cheater."

According to Dr. Williams, all three stages can damage you. In one study, high levels of hostility found in healthy men at age 25 were seen as predictors that they were up to seven times more likely to get heart disease or die by age 50.[5]

How can you tell if your man has a hostile heart that is headed for a heart attack? Dr. Williams proposes three questions that will raise a warning flag. Circle the answer that best represents the man in your life:

1. When anybody slows down or stops what he wants to do, he thinks they are selfish, mean, and inconsiderate.

Always   Often   Sometimes   Seldom   Never

2. When anybody does something that seems incompetent, messy, selfish, or inconsiderate to him, he quickly feels angry or enraged. At the same time, his heart races, his breath comes quickly, and his palms sweat.

Always   Often   Sometimes   Seldom   Never

3. When he has such thoughts or feelings, he lets fly with words, gestures, a raised voice, and frowns.

Always   Often   Sometimes   Seldom   Never

Dr. Williams says that if you answer *Often* or *Always* to two of the above questions, your man is in a high-risk heart group. Psychologists and psychiatrists have always told their patients to let anger out because, they said, if you hold it in, you can become depressed or develop ulcers. Williams gives quite another prescription: Help your man avoid *feeling* angry in the first place, and he won't need to suppress his anger.[6]

Ending It All

For an increasing number of men like Frank, Joe, and Karl, the ultimate and final expression of anger is suicide. The suicide rate among men, which is 300 times greater than the rate among women, is a sobering testimony that unresolved masculine anger is destroying great numbers of men today. And for each man who ends his life in frustration and despair, there is often a woman and some children who are personally, and sometimes permanently, devastated.

As you have traced the roots, reality, and results of masculine anger in the previous chapters, you may have recognized some disturbing patterns in your own man. And you may sense a degree of fear as you wonder about the toll his anger has already taken on him or may take on him, you, and your children in the future.

Don't push the panic button. Your angry man needs your help, whether he knows it or admits it or not.

There is hope. We present suggestions in the chapters ahead, but they are not a quick fix. It took years for the anger in a man to take root and grow. It will undoubtedly take some time for him to identify the issues and begin to deal with them properly. But we need to begin — carefully.

Think about It, Talk about It with Him

1. Men are usually composites of the four ways of expressing anger illustrated in this chapter. What percentage of the time would you estimate your man expresses his anger like each of the characters in the opening story?

____ % of the time he's like hot-headed Frank who expressed his anger in rage.

____ % of the time he's like vodka-swigging Joe who expressed his anger by displacing it in compulsive/addictive behavior.

____ % of the time he's like tight-lipped Karl who suppressed his anger.

____ % of the time he's like ready-to-talk Stan who worked through his anger constructively with his wife.

2. Has his expressions of rage resulted in any of the following problems for him? Explain.

a. Poisoned relationships at home.

b. Poisoned relationships at work.

c. Physical violence.

d. Sexual violence.

3. Has his displacement of anger resulted in any of the following problems for him? Explain.

a. Substance addiction, including money.

b. Sexual addiction.

c. Religious addiction.

4. Has his suppression of anger resulted in any of the following problems for him? Explain.

a. Symptoms of physical illness.

b. Thoughts or threats of suicide.

PART II

Resolving His Anger
and Finding Peace

6

Becoming His
Greatest Fan

Remember Cliff, the fearless killer of lawn mowers we met in Chapter 1? Thankfully, his story has a happy ending. Cliff's angry explosion that day—which was rather mild in comparison to the explosive reactions of some men—not only frightened Janice, his wife, but it frightened him. Fortunately, it frightened them into positive action. Within a few hours of the incident on the back lawn, Janice was able to say to Cliff, "Honey, I don't understand why you shot the lawn mower. The whole thing frightens me. I need us to talk about it."

Cliff wasn't sure how Janice would react. He kind of expected her to chew him out for such an irresponsible, costly, and dangerous display of anger. But when she approached him in such a positive manner, he realized that she wanted to be his ally in helping him deal with what he'd done and how he felt.

Later that evening, after the children had gone to bed, Cliff responded by trying to describe to Janice the feelings that led up to the lawn mower incident. He talked about the pressures and disappointments at work. Janice listened patiently. He described the distance he felt in their relationship and his struggle with loneliness. She kept listening respectfully and asking clarifying questions.

After about an hour of conversation, Cliff and Janice weren't much closer to understanding exactly how the feelings he described tied into the shooting of the lawn mower. For example, Cliff was unaware at this point how much his anger was the result of growing up without a strong father/mentor in his life. Nor was he thinking about how much the cultural myths of masculinity had pressured him to adopt career goals that often blocked him from having his personal needs met.

But at the end of their discussion, Cliff and Janice were closer to each other. As a result, they kept talking. In the weeks ahead, Cliff, with Janice by his side, sought professional counseling and came to terms with his anger.

The Woman Who Makes a Difference

In order to make a difference with your husband, you need to understand how he views his relationship with women in general and with you. The average man senses he is fully masculine only when he can attract women. And he must not only attract a woman but win one for himself alone as a wife or potential wife. As such, he unwittingly gives the women in his life terrifying power over him. Therefore, a man can be utterly deflated by a woman who refuses to be satisfied by him.

A dissatisfied or angry woman makes a man feel less than masculine and terrifies him. He has learned from his peers that if his woman is unhappy he has not been masculine enough. So he responds to her refusal, dissatisfaction, or anger by trying to generate even more masculinity, sometimes even becoming violent in his efforts to show enough masculinity to please his woman.

More than anything, he needs to know that you are on his side, that you're not against him. You need to communicate, more than you probably think necessary, that you accept him and love him, even though you may not be satisfied with some of his behaviors or responses. Separate the actions from the man, and affirm the man. His search for peace may begin sooner if he knows that you are satisfied with him and willing to walk with him through the steps of healing.

In this chapter we will share seven practical guidelines which you can use to be a positive, helpful instrument in your man's quest for peace from his anger. In a nutshell, these suggestions outline how you can show your man that you're for him, not against him. Author Fay Angus illustrates this concept by describing her relationship with her husband, John: "My commitment is to make John happy, and his commitment is to make me happy. He's my best cheerleader, and I'm his."[1] A key in helping your husband defuse his anger is assuring him that you are his greatest fan and best cheerleader.

Be His Friend, Not His Mother

Trudy and Phil have been married nine years, and they both work full time. Phil's high-stress job in the intensely competitive computer industry requires a lot of overtime. Like many men, much of his self-worth is tied up in his success and advancement at work, and he often comes home stressed out and angry.

Trudy spends many evenings just trying to help Phil feel better about himself and his job. She fixes him a nice dinner, draws him a hot bath, cleans up the kitchen while he relaxes in the tub, then listens to him complain about work until it's time for bed — all after she has put in a hard day at work herself.

In the morning, Phil tends to ignore the alarm, so Trudy must wake him several times while getting herself ready for work. She irons his shirt, picks out a matching tie and socks, and makes his breakfast. If he doesn't leave for work on time, she calls his secretary to tell her he'll be late.

Phil calls Trudy two or three times a week asking her to intercede between him and a difficult client or coworker, insisting, "You're so much better at people problems, Trudy." And Trudy, thinking that she is doing her part to help her man deal with the stress and anger in his life, does whatever he asks.

Trudy is doing Phil no favors by trailing after him like a mother. He doesn't need a mother; he needs a friend who will treat him, and insist on being treated by him, as an equal. He needs a friend who will gladly share life's responsibilities with him but not live his life for him, someone who will encourage him in his problem-solving but not solve all his problems for him.

Trudy occupies a mothering role in their marriage because that's the role she allowed Phil to push her into. In the absence of a strong father/mentor, Phil was over-mothered as a child. Mom did everything, fixed everything, picked up everything, and solved everything for him. He married Trudy as a romantic partner, but gradually returned to the role of the helpless, needy child to the extent that Trudy finally accepted the role of his make-everything-all-better mother.

If you find yourself playing a mothering role to your man, he will never fully deal with the causes and crises of his anger. The scared little boy in him will whine and fuss until you make it all better. You can transition from mother to friend in his life by lovingly placing in his hands those responsibilities and problems that he should deal with.

Appreciate Him, Don't Nag Him

It is estimated that upwards to 90 percent of all men today are unhappy and angry in their jobs to some degree. Our culture deifies men who own their own businesses and master their own fate in the world of employment and finance. But these men are the minority 10 percent, and the other 90 percent work for them. The 10 percent tells the 90 percent what to do and controls their hours and pay scale. They are subject to lay-offs, wage freezes, poor working conditions, transfers, and demotions. Most of them feel lucky to be working, but they often languish in their dead-end jobs feeling less than fully masculine because they are not in control of their own lives.

Much of the frustration among the 90 percent comes from the realization that the breaks have gone against them. "The boss isn't as smart or even as experienced as I am," they grouse. "He's just luckier than I am. He just happened to be in the right place at the right time. His father knew the owner." Or they say, "The only reason he owns this company is because his parents bought it for him. If I came from a wealthy family, I'd be a boss instead of a peon."

It's likely that a significant portion of your man's anger springs from a sense of lack of control in his work. Nagging him to buck for promotions or beg for raises may only intensify his anger. Bugging him for a bigger house or a newer car may only deepen his frustration that he has no more control at home than he has on the job. But if you become a wellspring of appreciation for the work that he does and the living he provides, you will lift some of the pressure from his life. Find many ways to say to him, "I appreciate that you work hard at your job and that you hang in there even when it's frustrating and tough. I couldn't love you more if you owned the whole company."

Affirm Him, Don't Criticize Him

Some men are not only upset because they must work for someone else but because of the kind of work they must do. James is a college-trained engineer who can't find a job in his chosen field. So he resorted to the management training program of a fast-food chain. The job helps pay the bills, but James is embarrassed about being the crew chief in an assembly-line taco stand. He hasn't stopped looking for an engineering position, but he's afraid that he's trapped in what he considers a menial, degrading job.

LaVonne, James' wife, is a real breath of fresh air in his life. She continues to affirm him as a talented and useful employee. "You're an excellent engineer, Honey," she tells him.

"The world just hasn't discovered you yet. You're too good and too well-trained to be overlooked for long. In the meantime, the taco place is lucky to have you. You're such a competent, conscientious manager." LaVonne is committed to affirm James no matter what his job may be. If he decided to make the fast-food industry his career, she would be his greatest fan.

If your man is struggling with being locked into a job that is distasteful to him, you can ease his struggle by affirming him for who he is and what he does. Compliment him for the character qualities he exercises (or needs to exercise) in his job: patience, perseverance, determination, creativity, etc. In everything you say and do, let him know that he is the best taco maker (or pump jockey, accountant, construction worker, sanitation engineer, etc.) in the world. Appreciate him for the effort, not for the results.

Give Him Space, Don't Crowd Him

Imagine how Cliff would have responded after shooting the lawn mower if Janice had taken this approach:

She follows him back to the den demanding that he tell her what's wrong with him, and continues to bug him about it through the evening. She rushes down to the bookstore and buys a stack of self-help books for him to read. Not content to let him read at his own pace, she reads to him at mealtimes and bedtime. She calls the church to alert the prayer chain about his "problem" and to ask the pastor to come see him. She drags him off to hear special speakers in hopes that someone will be able to turn him around. Whenever they're with friends, she brings up his problem and asks them to give him advice.

If Cliff is like most men, he wouldn't have put up with Janice's constant pestering for long. He would have tuned her out emotionally or bailed out physically. He may even have lashed out at her in a hurtful way like a cornered animal.

Most of us don't like to be pushed, especially men. It's an affront to their struggling masculinity and only serves to exacerbate their anger. They feel intimidated because their wives can't accept them the way they are. They feel inferior in comparison to the ideal man their wives are badgering them to become. Once again they are not in control of their own lives.

Give your husband plenty of room. Show him that you're concerned about him and that you love him. Let him know that you're available to listen to him and talk to him. Then *back off* to pray and wait. Trust God to work for your man's good in the situation. Allow Him to use "the unfading beauty of a gentle and quiet spirit" (1 Peter 3:4) in you to encourage and help him.

Pushing your man to solve his anger may cause him to make some cursory changes to get you off his back. But pressure from you is not likely to produce a lasting solution. When you step back and give God room to work, the changes will be significant and enduring.

Give Him Time, Don't Rush Him

We live in the age of instant gratification. Thanks to modern technology we travel thousands of miles in hours instead of days. We cook meals in minutes instead of hours. We can solve problems and transact business in seconds with our high speed computers, car phones, and cable shopping channels. Like no other culture to date, we hate to wait.

The subconscious urgency we all share for fast results may get in the way, however, when it comes to the process of helping a man defuse his anger. The family and cultural causes for his anger may have been eating at him for years, possibly for decades. The dysfunctional patterns and harmful habits he employs to express his anger are no doubt deeply ingrained. These things don't change overnight. It may take him weeks, months, and even years to fully heal from the causes and results of anger in his life. (Miracles do happen, of course, but they are usually the exception and not the rule.).

One word of caution, however: If you have reason to believe that you or your children are in imminent physical danger from angry outbursts, you need to take some steps to protect yourself and them. Talk to your pastor or to a counselor. If necessary, find a place to stay where you can feel safe.

Hold Him Responsible, Don't Be Co-dependent

Eddie's temper got him into trouble at work on a number of occasions. He verbally popped off to his boss by contradicting his orders and undermined his leadership by bad-mouthing him to other employees. Finally Eddie was notified that he was on probation, in danger of termination if he crossed the boss again.

When Eddie told his wife Angela about the incident, she secretly went to see his boss. "I'm sorry for Eddie's displays of anger," she said. "It's really my fault. I haven't been the best wife I can be, and the kids have been on his nerves lately. If you'll just forgive him, I'll try to turn things around at home so this won't happen again." Eddie's boss was sympathetic and rescinded the probation.

Again Eddie's expression of anger pushed the wrong buttons at work, and he was placed on probation for a second time. Again Angela pleaded with the boss to give Eddie another chance, which he refused to do. Within days Eddie's angry words cost him his job.

For Angela, the solution to the problem was obvious. She was able to get a full-time job where she worked before their three young children were born. She makes considerably less money than Eddie did, and child-care expenses eat up much of it. They are behind on most of their bills. Eddie's bad reputation in the industry has resulted in his application for employment at several companies being denied. Angela is now looking for a part-time evening job.

If his anger gets him into trouble in any way, you are not responsible to cover for him or take the rap for him. Doing so only allows the problem to continue; it never stops the problem. Only when we allow someone to face the consequences of his behavior will he begin to see that he is responsible for making changes in the way he behaves.

The more Angela did to cover for Eddie, the worse things became. The harder she worked to cover the bills, the less Eddie had to do to be responsible. It's not easy to stop covering for someone like Eddie, and usually a support group will be necessary to help Angela have to the strength and determination to stay out of Eddie's problems. But until she does seek help, Eddie's anger won't diminish — it will continue to grow.

Give to Him, Don't Withhold from Him

If your husband is in the process of dealing with expressions of anger that have been hurtful to you in some way, you may be tempted to say something like, "Once you get your act together, then I'll start being the wife I should be." You may feel like withholding affection or sex from him until he "deserves" it. You may feel like asking him to move out until he has better control of his temper or habits. Or he may have troubled you so much that you are ready to give up on him all together.

While there are a few occasions when a temporary separation may be necessary (such as when his uncontrolled rage is endangering you or the children), you can probably be more helpful to your man's healing by staying with him. Love, forgiveness, and acceptance are qualities to be given freely, not to be held as hostages for ransom. He needs your friendship, not your judgment. God will use your openness, kindness, and willingness to go the second mile to aid in his healing.

Hope on the Horizon

You may be wondering, "If I become his greatest fan and best cheerleader, what results can I expect in him?" First, you will build in him a quality that is indispensible if you are to be an instrument of helpfulness in his healing: trust. He must trust you if he is going to let you help him. He must trust that you have his best interests at heart. He must trust that you will not hurt him or embarrass him intentionally. He must trust that you will stay with him through the long haul. Only when he trusts, will he be free to share with you the entire gamut of feelings that may be perpetuating his anger.

Second, hopefully your commitment to love, accept, encourage, affirm, and forgive your man will become a sturdy bridge between his angry heart and what Dr. Redford Williams of the Duke University Medical Center calls "a trusting heart." In his book, *The Trusting Heart,* Dr. Williams contends that hostility begins with the mistrust of others and is reduced by developing a trusting heart. Your commitment to be his greatest fan will help free him to take Dr. Williams' twelve steps for acquiring feelings of trust:

1. He monitors cynical thoughts by recognizing them.
2. He confesses his hostility and seeks support for change.
3. He stops cynical thoughts.
4. He reasons with himself.
5. He puts himself in the other guy's shoes.
6. He laughs at himself.
7. He practices relaxing.
8. He tries trusting others.
9. He forces himself to listen more.
10. He substitutes aggressiveness (firmness) for aggression.
11. He pretends that today is his last day.
12. He practices forgiveness.[2]

As you begin to understand the roots of his anger and lovingly support him and cheer him on as he deals with his anger, you will begin to see these characteristics increasing. Your encouragement and affirmation will help build his trust in you and his confidence in partnering with you to find the peace he seeks.

Think about It, Talk about It with Him

1. How would you grade your success at practicing the guidelines presented in this chapter? Circle the appropriate grade for each, then write one sentence explaining the reason for the grade you selected.

Be his friend, not his mother.

A+ A A-   B+ B B-   C+ C C-   D+ D D- F

Appreciate him, don't nag him.

A+ A A-   B+ B B-   C+ C C-   D+ D D- F

Affirm him, don't criticize him.

A+ A A-   B+ B B-   C+ C C-   D+ D D- F

Give him space, don't crowd him.

A+ A A-   B+ B B-   C+ C C-   D+ D D- F

Give him time, don't rush him.

A+ A A-   B+ B B-   C+ C C-   D+ D D- F

Hold him responsible, don't be co-dependent.

A+ A A-   B+ B B-   C+ C C-   D+ D D- F

Give to him, don't withhold from him.

A+ A A-   B+ B B-   C+ C C-   D+ D D- F

2. Select one guideline for which you graded yourself lower than for some others. What can you do this week to begin positive follow-through on this guideline?

3. To what degree does your husband have a hostile heart? A trusting heart? For each statement below circle a number between 0-10 representing the presence of that quality in his life (0 means "he never does this," 10 means "he always does this," etc.).

He monitors cynical thoughts by recognizing them.

0   1   2   3   4   5   6   7   8   9   10

He confesses his hostility and seeks support for change.

0   1   2   3   4   5   6   7   8   9   10

He stops cynical thoughts.

0   1   2   3   4   5   6   7   8   9   10

He reasons with himself.

0   1   2   3   4   5   6   7   8   9   10

He puts himself in the other guy's shoes.

0   1   2   3   4   5   6   7   8   9   10

He laughs at himself.

0   1   2   3   4   5   6   7   8   9   10

He practices relaxing.

0   1   2   3   4   5   6   7   8   9   10

He tries trusting others.

0   1   2   3   4   5   6   7   8   9   10

He forces himself to listen more.

0   1   2   3   4   5   6   7   8   9   10

He substitutes aggressiveness (firmness) for aggression.

0   1   2   3   4   5   6   7   8   9   10

He pretends that today is his last day.

0   1   2   3   4   5   6   7   8   9   10

He practices forgiveness.

0   1   2   3   4   5   6   7   8   9   10

7

Answering the Questions of Manhood

By all outward appearances, 56-year-old Tony is a very successful man. He nets about $1 million a year from his real es-
tate development business in southern California. He shares a
$3 million beach-front home with his second wife, young and
beautiful Della, and their three-year-old adopted daughter,
Tiffany. He enjoys all the "toys" that most men his age only
dream about: luxury cars, yacht, world travel, expensive suits,
fine jewelry, and a fat stock portfolio. Tony is set for life.

But for all his apparent success, Tony is a frustrated, depressed, angry man. So he went to see a psychologist. "What
do you want to do with the rest of your life, Tony?" the psychologist asked after Tony vented some of his
negative feelings.

"I'm lining up a series of mall sites for a major developer
in the east," Tony answered, suddenly animated as he spoke
of his dream. "It might take me a couple of years to tie it up,

but it could be the deal of a lifetime. I want to hit it big once more. I could walk away from this one with $5 million."

The counselor replied, "What are you going to do with another $5 million? You already have more money than you know what to do with, and it's not making you happy. Aren't you ready to slow down a little and smell the flowers?"

"That's what my ex tried to get me to do for 20 years," Tony snapped. "But I wouldn't be where I am today if I'd have taken her advice. So I just smiled at her and kept working until I couldn't take her incessant harping anymore; then I divorced her. I thought Della would be different. When we met she was young and full of adventure. But soon after we were married she started bugging me about adopting. I finally gave in hoping she and the baby would leave me to my work. But now Della's talking about family vacations abroad. She wants me to watch Tiffany a couple of days a week while she goes out. I'm not ready for that. I've got too much to do. I probably won't be able to keep smiling in this marriage as long as I did in the first one."

Tony's dilemma is common to many men. At 53, instead of focusing on his relationships and enjoying the fruits of his labor, he is still trying to prove to himself that he is a man of competence and worth. At a time in life when he should be recognizing his limitations and down-scaling his life to accommodate them, he's still trying to hit it big.

Tony is a frustrated, angry man because he's been asking vital questions about his role as a man for about 35 years and no one has provided adequate answers. So he has spent most of his life scrabbling fruitlessly for some clue about his identity and purpose. His sense of futility has already destroyed one marriage and is poised to sink another.

Unanswered Questions

There are five questions men ask about the masculine role in life. If a man fails to find the right answers to these questions, he will be frustrated and angry like Tony regardless of how great his career or financial success may be. And he will likely take his anger out on those closest to him, especially you. The questions are as follows:

1. Am I a man?
2. Am I competent?
3. Do I have worth beyond my paycheck?
4. Can I accept my limitations?
5. Do I have meaning beyond my accomplishments?

Ideally, a man is able to answer these questions about himself in the affirmative as they occur over the course of adulthood. Armed with a clear definition of his manhood, competence, worth, limitations, and meaning, he can live at peace with himself, be productive in his career, have his deepest emotional needs met, and be a source of nurture in all his relationships, especially with his wife.

Unfortunately, many men get stumped on the first question. They stumble through the first 7 or 8 years of their adult life trying to define true manhood and prove that they fit the description. Without a definitive answer, they move into the second stage of years grappling with the question of their competence as a man, the third stage trying to discover their worth beyond what they earn, and the fourth stage trying to come to terms with their limitations. By the time of retirement, many men are still not sure that their life has much meaning beyond what they have accomplished in the preceding 65 years. The five stages of unanswered questions look like this:

Stage 1:   Am I a man? (ages 18-25)
Stage 2:   Am I competent? (ages 26-40)
Stage 3:   Do I have worth beyond my paycheck?
             (ages 41-50)
Stage 4:   Can I accept my limitations? (ages 51-65)
Stage 5:   Do I have meaning beyond my accomplishments? (age 65+)

Every man must work through the five developmental stages in sequence. It's possible that, with the proper environment and examples, a man can come to grips with the truth about his manhood, competence, worth, limitations, and meaning in a matter of a few years. However, with the disappearance of the father/mentor in our culture, an increasing number of men are groping aimlessly through each stage. The process is painfully protracted because their fathers and grandfathers have run away with the correct answers, assuming they even knew the answers. All they have left to choose from are the multiple choice answers of mythical masculinity — and all those answers are wrong.

It's possible that your husband is struggling with anger because he's trying to get through life as a man without the answers he needs. Like Tony, he may reach mid-life or beyond still trying frantically to make his mark in the world because he doesn't understand that manhood is being somebody, not doing something.

As the woman in his life, you need to understand these five questions and the developmental stages men labor through when they don't know the right answers.

The following pages will equip you with a better understanding of the five stages and suggest practical ways by which you can help your husband find the right answers and move on. The sooner he comes to terms with his manhood, competence, worth, limitations, and meaning, the sooner his anger will be resolved and he will find peace.

Stage 1: Am I a Man? (Ages 18-25)

During an extended period of counseling, Tony's psychologist uncovered a primary source of Tony's anger. Tony's father died when he was a young boy. The event devastated him, and he plummeted into a depression that overtly lasted about a year.

Tony was finally able to push the depression aside through his achievements. He became an instant achiever, pouring himself into school work and athletics, and excelling in both. He went on to college and into business knowing nothing but success because of his commitment to hard work and achievement. He didn't know that his solution was temporary. As the oldest child, he had become super-responsible. It was like he had suddenly become an adult, only he was 11 at the time.

As a young man, Tony, somewhere deep inside him, asked himself, "Am I a man?" But he couldn't come up with an answer. His father, the main man in his life, was dead. Young Tony didn't know by example what a real man was. The question persisted: "Am I a man?" Without the example and instruction of his father, Tony saw the achievement-oriented men in his culture and deduced that a real man was someone who worked hard, earned lots of money, and climbed the ladder of success. In his mind, to be a man he had to achieve, he had to produce.

In his ignorance, Tony wrongly defined manhood as something he did, not something he was. He spent his whole life achieving. He couldn't stop producing, even at the expense of one marriage — and possibly two — because in his mind if he stopped producing he stopped being a real man. Any threat to his achievement was a threat to his manhood, and that kept him perpetually angry.

Like Tony, many men are stuck in Stage 1 throughout life because they don't really know what true masculinity is. Their fathers may have abandoned them physically or emotionally, providing little by way of father-to-son instruction and example. And if a boy's dad was physically and emotionally present during his childhood, the man may have modeled the mythical version of masculinity that his son unwittingly took for reality. Such boys are highly impressionable and vulnerable to the myths of masculinity rampant in our culture.

When a man's definition of masculinity is linked to doing something, he will answer the question "Am I a man?" with "I don't know" because he may not be sure that he's doing enough. And when he's incapable of "doing" for some reason (ill, laid off, etc.), his manhood is in jeopardy and his anxiety, frustration, fear, guilt, and anger increase.

Affirming His Manhood

During Stage 1 a man is in the process of assessing his strengths and weaknesses. For most men, the more strengths he finds, the more he feels like a man; the more weaknesses he finds, the less manly he feels. Here are some practical ways to help your husband resolve this first stage.

Show appreciation for who he is. Tell him often in conversation and in cards, letters, and notes that you love him just the way he is. Comment on the character qualities you appreciate in him. For example, one woman told her man, "It really turns me on when you I see you being so nice to our kids."

On the home front, watch for and compliment him for the little things he does to make your life together easier and more enjoyable. For example, if he likes to work outside, thank him for keeping the yard in such nice condition. If he's a fix-it man around the house, appreciate him for keeping the appliances working and changing the washers on the sink. If he is "all thumbs," acknowledge his other skills: preparing the income tax return, keeping track of the finances, the cleaning that he does, etc. When you appreciate him just as he is, you affirm his sense of "being" and this will help relieve the pressure he may feel to become something different or better.

Help him accept his weaknesses and failures. Whenever something needs to be fixed at Red and Trina's house, Red feels it's his responsibility to do the job. Trina's father was the fix-it man around her house growing up, so Red wants to live up to his example and his wife's expectations. The only problem is that Red is hopelessly inept at mechanical things—he is "all thumbs." Whenever he attempts a plumbing, electrical, auto, or appliance repair, he ends up going to the hardware store three or four times. First, he has to buy the right tool to remove the broken part. Then he goes back to buy the replacement part. He usually either comes home with the wrong size part or breaks it while installing it, so back to the store he goes again. When he's done, half the time he discovers that what he fixed wasn't the problem to begin with.

At each level of failure in this process Red gets angrier and angrier. He wants so badly to prove to Trina that he is every bit the man her father is. But his failures only further expose his mechanical ineptitude.

Trina is a wise woman, however. After Red recently went a few unsuccessful rounds with their water heater, she said, "Honey, I don't expect you to be the fix-it man that my father is anymore than I expect him to be the computer genius that you are. I appreciate your willingness to try to fix the water heater. But it's okay with me if we call a plumber to do the job. Your time is too valuable to be wasted doing something you hate when you have so many other things you do so well."

Strength and success are such high masculine values in our culture that many men feel less than manly when they discover a weakness or experience a failure. Like Red, feeling inept in an area where men are characteristically skilled makes him boiling mad. Other men feel the same response when they get laid off, when they can't improve their golf score, etc.

When your husband struggles with weakness or failure, you can help him keep a proper perspective. Remind him that, contrary to what he feels, failure is not the end of the world. Everybody fails, and he's no less a man because he does. Redirect his attention to his strengths and successes. Remind him of the points of strength others have noted in him. Never belittle him in private or in public for what he cannot do or has not accomplished. The less importance you attach to his weaknesses and failures — great or small — the easier it will be for him to let go of them.

Be content to live within your means. If you continually press your husband to live at an economic level that exceeds what the two of you can comfortably afford, you may be contributing to his anger. He wants to make you happy. But if you're always wishing for a larger house, more expensive furnishings, a more fashionable wardrobe, an exotic vacation, etc., he may think that his success as a man is contingent on providing for you the lifestyle you desire. He may feel pressured to find a better job, work longer hours, or go deeper into debt to fulfill your whims. His manhood is reduced to material and monetary terms.

There's nothing wrong with dreaming and planning *together* to better your life. But he needs to know that your happiness is centered in him, not in what the two of you can accumulate.

Help him dream realistic dreams. "I don't care how long it takes, I'm going to climb the corporate ladder and be president of this company some day. I'll have a corner office, a BMW or two, and a winter home in the islands. I'll come in at 10:00 A.M. and leave by 4:00 every day, except when I take off earlier to play golf."

Lots of men begin their careers like this — with stars in their eyes. They think that rising to the top of their company or field is the ultimate demonstration of their manhood. But while goals are good, grandiose ideas of conquest like the one above are not only unrealistic but ultimately deflating. It takes more than a big dream and a lot of want-to to be a company president. Many men have burned themselves out climbing the stairway to the stars only to discover when they reach their fifties that they just don't have what it takes to reach the top. These men are often devastated because their success as a man is hinged on their success at realizing their dream.

Help your husband keep his feet on the ground by confronting his grandiose ideas and encouraging him to dream realistically. Assure him that you will love him no more if he becomes company president than you did when he was a mail room clerk. If he must aim so high, challenge him to set reachable short-term goals: assistant mail room manager, mail room manager, mail room supervisor, etc. Then celebrate each of his achievements.

Stage 2: Am I Competent? (Ages 26-40)

Angry men are often the personification of the old quip, "Being unsure of our goals, we redoubled our efforts." They desperately want to prove to themselves and the world that they are men, even though they're not quite sure what a real man is. So regardless of their blurred focus and feelings of inadequacy, they set out to show that they're the best at what they do. In reality, they just want someone to tell them what they likely never heard from their fathers: "Good job, young man!" Men striving to prove their competency often have a hard time accepting their limits. They feel driven to conquer. They are the workaholics of society, working themselves to death (many of them literally!) trying to cover their feelings of inadequacy with a thick veneer of accomplishment. And their drive to establish competency in the workplace often damages their competency in the home.

Affirming His Competency

If your husband is going to find peace from his anger, he needs to answer the question "Am I competent?" in the affirmative. If he can't affirm his competency he may end up working himself into a heart attack.

Here are some tips you can use to affirm your husband's competency.

Acknowledge his achievements. Congratulate him for his victories — even his smallest ones — as you would if he had won the president's chair. Point out that he has done more than you expected. Comment on his achievements to others and encourage them to recognize him for his accomplishments. The more affirmation he receives for even his small victories, the less need he will feel to prove his competency.

One area of competency in which he may be especially vulnerable to self-doubt is his sexual performance. Most men equate successful masculinity with successful sex. If he thinks he's failing at love-making, he will have to redouble his efforts to prove himself competent. Affirm his sexual competence. Tell him about the techniques he employs that you really like.

Forgive him for his failures. Imagine that Trina was unwilling to forgive Red for botching a repair job around the home.

She used his incompetence as ammunition in every argument and humiliated him in front of their friends with stories of broken parts and misused tools. What would Red's response be?

With his failures being dangled mercilessly in front of his face, Red likely would have redoubled his efforts to prove his competence. He may have taken on more repair projects just to prove to Trina that he could do them. And his repeated failures probably would have spawned an even deeper attitude of anger.

Instead of criticizing him, forgive him for his failures. Remind him that his failures in a project, relationship, or job cast no shadow on his inherent value as a person. Then give him enough space to try again or find another niche. Keep reminding him that he is much more important to you than anything he does.

Let your unconditional love flow to him. Your husband should find in you an emotional respite from the dog-eat-dog world he works in every day. Your acceptance and forgiveness should provide a safe haven from those who are out to knock him off the corporate ladder as they scramble their way to the top. Help him feel secure in your strength and stability. When he finds you to be someone who loves, forgives, and accepts him no matter what, his need to prove his manhood and competence will diminish.

Stage 3: Do I Have Worth Beyond My Paycheck? (Ages 41-50)

At age 56, Tony was financially secure. He could retire on his investments and live comfortably — albeit not quite as luxuriously — on the interest. But Tony's score card of personal worth has always had dollar signs on it. He had wooed and won two of the loveliest women in California with his money. He was accepted in a large circle of influential, wealthy friends simply because he had attained a seven-digit income. Now, given the choice between nurturing his new family and hitting it big in business again, Tony's score card of personal worth takes over. Everything he's learned about manhood urges him to go for the dollars, because a man is nothing without money.

The same psychologist who is seeing Tony is seeing Bruce. At age 48, Bruce is in at a similar crossroads in his career as Tony is. Bruce spent 20 years building up a business that he sold to a Japanese investment group for $6 million. He has a contract with the new owners that will allow him to stay on as president of the company. With a fresh injection of money in the company, Bruce could easily double his income in the first year.

The psychologist asked Bruce the same question he asked Tony: "What are you going to do with more money? You already have more money than you know what to do with." They talked together about the importance of Bruce's relationship with his wife and children, and of the time away from home his new position would require. Gradually Bruce decided that his worth to himself and his family could not be measured in digits on a paycheck. He took a job as a part-time consultant to the new owners and turned toward nurturing his relationships with family and friends.

By the time they're well into mid-life, men who have been struggling to prove their manhood and competence begin asking a third series of questions: "Do I have worth beyond my paycheck?" "Am I loved for who I am or just for my current market value?" "Does my family love and respect me for more than the shelter and food my earnings provide?"

Up to this point in their lives, men like Tony and Bruce have felt that they have earned love from family and friends through their career successes. But as they walk into their fifties, they can see the end of the trail. They can envision the day when their career dreams will be beyond reach. And they feel fearful and angry because they think their manhood will go down the drain with their ability to earn a good paycheck. Your husband can use your help if he is to answer this question correctly.

Affirming His Worth

One of the main reasons Bruce could walk away from a lucrative business proposition at age 48 is his wife, Steffie. Over the years she has generously affirmed Bruce's manhood, competence, and worth apart from what he does or how much he earns. Steffie has enjoyed the fruits of Bruce's success, but she has been careful to communicate that she loves him for who he is, not for what he does or how much he earns. Steffie's affirmation was probably the telling vote in Bruce's decision not to plunge back into the company he had just sold.

You need to assure him that he is of infinitely greater worth to you and others than the numbers on his paycheck. Your affirmation could bridge the gap between his fading career dreams and a new dream that is not founded on material success.

Accept his disappointment. Your husband may be disappointed, discouraged, and angry that he has not reached the financial goals he set for himself when he embarked on his career. His disappointment may be even greater when he realizes that he never will earn what he thinks he's worth in the job market.

Allow him to vent his anger at not doing all he wanted to do and earning as much as he thought he could. Assure him that your score card for him is not based on dollar signs but on the positive character traits he exhibits, especially in your relationship.

Show your respect for his unique abilities. There's much more to him than the skills he uses to earn a living. Look carefully for the qualities he possesses that transcend the business setting. For example, thank him for all he does to nourish your relationship (even if some of his abilities are weak or dormant): his conversation skills, his nonverbal caring and affection, his lovemaking skills, etc. Verbally acknowledge his abilities with children: his playfulness, his willingness to feed, change, bathe, and bed down an infant, his consistency in discipline, etc. Remind him that these important abilities will remain even when his business skills are no longer in use.

Help him find new dreams to replace the old. As Bruce struggled with his new role as consultant to a company he once owned, his wife, Steffie, recognized new skills of helpfulness emerging in him. At her encouragement, Bruce got involved in the fund-raising committee of the local children's hospital. Today he is the chairman of that committee. While he still misses being at the helm of his old business, Bruce's new dream of raising funds to build a wing on the hospital has become his passion.

In order to defuse the anger brought on by the dissolution of a lifelong career dream, he needs a new dream, one that reflects who he is, not so much what he can earn. Your affirmation of his various qualities and skills can help bring his new dream into focus.

Stage 4: Can I Accept My Limitations? (Ages 51-65)

Men like Tony mistakenly believe that they will keep turning big deals and earning big bucks as they sail into the sunset of their lives. They want to leave this earth revered, respected, and praised for their position and accomplishments. They refuse to accept the fact that they will eventually reach a point when their physical energy and business acumen will recede. In short, they refuse to accept their limitations — present and future — because to them such an admission is a compromise of their manhood. And when they are overcome by their limitations, they are confused, depressed, and angry as a result. This is one reason why so many men die within the first few years of retirement. Their work was their life, and since they can no longer cut it at work, they give up on life.

Men like Bruce, however, have come to terms with the realization that they are not invincible and that they can't do everything. They have accepted the reality of aging and are thinking sensibly about what they need to do before they die.

Affirming His Limitations

How can you help your husband resolve this stage like Bruce instead of Tony? Here are some suggestions.

Assist him in overcoming his limitations. Some men blame their limitations on age as a cop out. For example, he may say he's too old to play racquetball when he's not too old, just overweight and out of shape. Encourage him to get into a conditioning program (many community colleges and hospitals sponsor them for a nominal charge) and enjoy the sport while he can.

On the other hand, he may be in excellent condition for his age, but he still can't compete on a par with the 25-year-olds on the court. Assure him that his ability is normal for his age and that you think no less of him because of his limitations. Help him find new interests and hobbies that fit his abilities and interests. For example, he may never again win the racquetball championship, but he could still be a contender at target shooting, bridge, pool, or golf.

Don't hold a grudge over faded dreams. You may have been caught up in your husband's unrealistic goals of business success and its accompanying rewards. He may have promised you a big house in the country, furs, jewels, vacations, etc., and you bought into it. Now as you help him adjust to his limitations you are tempted to feel bitter because he will never be able to deliver on these promises.

If you hold a grudge over your husband's faded dreams you will only push him deeper into his depression and anger. You need to accept his limitations, be content with what you have, and not exacerbate his anger by whining over what he didn't give you. Don't allow any negative talk about limitations from him or yourself. Your accepting, positive attitude will help him deal appropriately with his limitations and faded dreams.

Encourage him to remain social. Men tend to pull away from other people during this stage. They look at their peers and see a mirror image of themselves glaring at them with all the limitations they find so difficult to accept. They avoid younger people because young adults only remind them of the youth they have lost. And they don't like being with older adults because they represent even more limitations to be faced in the years ahead.

Every man needs to avoid the temptation to retreat into himself at this time. Find new ways to enjoy your time together as a couple: taking trips, playing games, walking, dating each other, etc. Help him find new hobbies and interests that will keep him involved with other people. Suggest that you take a night class together in pottery, horticulture, CPR, or a subject you both like. Get involved in a church or adult Bible study group together. Host dinner parties for friends and new acquaintances of all ages, and involve your man in all stages of the evening. The more you can involve him with people, the less time he will have to sit around and feel sorry about not being as productive as he once was.

Stage 5: Do I Have Meaning Beyond My Accomplishments? (Age 65+)

At the height of his career as an assembly line foreman for an automobile manufacturing plant, Rod felt that his life had real meaning. Sixteen people on his shift depended on him while on the job. Rod felt that his work was a significant part of a greater whole. Without the hoods and trunk lids his team installed, the cars would be incomplete. He was confident that there were few men in the plant who could do his job as skillfully as he did. He knew that if he died suddenly he would be sorely missed by his coworkers and superiors at the plant as well as by his family.

But Rod is now 66. He's retired from the plant, and someone just as competent is running the hood and trunk crew efficiently. Rod realizes that he's no longer needed on the assembly line. What's more, Rod realizes that he isn't needed by his family either. His children are grown and gone. He hears from them briefly on holidays. His wife is in poor health, but a home-care nurse tends to her needs three times a week. He wonders if anybody will show up at his funeral or miss him when he's gone.

Affirming His Meaning. Rod needs assurance of his meaning and importance now that he is no longer working or providing for a family. Many men like Rod approach this stage looking for meaning in life beyond their past accomplishments. There are several ways you can help him on this point.

Help him find a new life mission. An older man without a mission becomes easily despondent, especially if his working years have been productive and meaningful to him. He needs to find another outlet for his talents that will give him a sense of purpose. In most cities there are many paid and volunteer positions where the stability and maturity of a senior adult is preferred. Sixty-nine-year-old Oliver works as a crossing guard near an elementary school. He only works two or three hours a day, but since he started his life has new meaning, and he's gaining some new friends among the children he sees every day.

There are also many projects a man can take on besides formal volunteer or paid positions. Fred, 90, a former real estate commissioner for the state of California, goes to a nearby nursing home every day to visit his wife for a couple of hours. He also walks into all the rooms and warmly greets the patients, some of whom receive no other visitors. Fred's business and government accomplishments are far behind him, but he still finds meaning in life as he brings joy and love to the patients he visits every day. Your husband may need your help in finding places of meaningful activity as Oliver and Fred have.

Assure him of your love. As his career ends and his feelings of uselessness and purposelessness run rampant, he may wonder if your love for him has stood the test of time. Communicate your love and friendship in numbers of ways. For example, look through the family photo album together and reminisce about the good times of the past. As you do, assure him that your love and respect for him is just as strong as ever. Tell him that you still lean on him for emotional support and friendship. Your affirmation of love will remind him that his life still has at least one significant purpose: caring for you.

Forgive his failures. Your husband may have quirks and habits that have bugged you throughout your life together. He may have done or said things that hurt you deeply. He may have spent money irresponsibly or failed in business. No matter what your man has done or become that is offensive to you, Stage 5 is not the time to try to remake him. Holding grudges or trying to punish him or whip him into shape will only make things worse. It's time to forgive him for his failures and focus on making your life together as harmonious and fruitful as possible.

Think about It, Talk about It with Him

1. What stage is your husband in? Underline the stage he may be in due to his age (i.e., if he is 35, underline Stage 2, etc.). Then circle the stage he appears to be in by the kinds of activities in which he's presently involved.

    Stage 1:   Am I a man? (ages 18-25)

    Stage 2:   Am I competent? (ages 26-40)

    Stage 3:   Do I have worth beyond my paycheck? (ages 41-50)

    Stage 4:   Can I accept my limitations? (ages 51-65)

    Stage 5:   Do I have meaning beyond my accomplishments? (age 65+)

2. Affirming his manhood: Select at least one of the suggestions below, and write a one- or two-sentence note to your husband in which you affirm his manhood as suggested. Do the same for affirming his competence, worth, limitations, and meaning.

Show appreciation for who he is and what he does.

Help him accept his weaknesses and failures.

Be content to live within your means.

Help him dream realistic dreams.

3. Affirming his competency.

Acknowledge his achievements.

Forgive him for his failures.

Let your unconditional love flow to him.

4. Affirming his worth.

   Accept his disappointment.

   Show your respect for his unique abilities.

   Help him find new dreams to replace the old.

5. Affirming his limitations.

   Assist him in overcoming his limitations.

   Don't hold a grudge over faded dreams.

   Encourage him to remain social.

6. Affirming his meaning.

   Help him find a new life mission.

   Assure him of your love.

   Forgive his failures.

   7. Look back over the brief notes you have written. Take a separate sheet of paper or a card and blend these notes into a brief letter of affirmation to your husband that you will mail to his office or slip under his pillow.

8

Talking It Over Together

Jake stormed into the house like a hurricane hitting the shore. "Why is the garage door standing open, and why are my tools spread out all over the floor?" he blustered angrily as he slammed the front door and stomped toward the kitchen.

Marian, who had only been home from work about ten minutes herself, was in the basement loading the washer. "Jake, I'm downstairs," she called out. Then she heard the exaggerated *clomp-clomp-clomp* of Jake's work boots above her as he marched through the kitchen to the basement staircase.

"Philip knows better than to leave the garage door open," Jake grumbled as he tramped down the stairs. "My tools are expensive, and he's practically inviting the neighborhood vandals to walk in and help themselves." Jake greeted his wife in the basement with a little kiss, but the scowl never left his face.

"Philip was in the garage working on his motorcycle when I got home a few minutes ago," Marian explained as she tossed the last of the "darks" into the washer. "He's probably out road-testing it. I'm sure he'll be right back."

"It doesn't take long for one of the little thieves around here to lift a set of wrenches," Jake said, hands on hips in a posture of indignation. "So I closed the garage door and locked it. Philip will have to deal with me if he wants to work on his bike now."

Marian was suspicious that Jake's outburst had a deeper root than Philip's thoughtlessness. "How were things at the shop today?" she asked as she sat down on a large, inverted bucket near the washer.

Jake relaxed a little at her question and leaned against a post that supported the upper floors. "Pretty lousy for a Friday," he snorted. "I got stuck on the lathe all day because Tex didn't show up. So Danny and Mike had to do all my stapling, and I'm not sure they did a very good job. I'll probably have to go in tomorrow for a few hours to undo and redo what they tried to do."

"But you and your dad are going duck hunting this weekend. I just put your favorite flannel shirt into the washer so you can wear it tomorrow."

"Won't need it," Jake said, standing straight and rigid again with his arms crossed. "We're not going."

"Not going? You've been planning this weekend trip for two months. Are you really going to let a bad stapling job keep you from –."

"Dad cancelled the trip," Jake interrupted. "He called me at the shop this afternoon and said, 'Sorry, but my schedule has changed and I can't go.'"

"Oh, Honey. I'm sorry," Marian said as she stood up and touched his arm. "You were really looking forward to this trip. How do you feel about the trip being cancelled?" Marian already knew how her husband was feeling, but she had learned how important it was for both of them that she ask.

"It's just like when I was a kid." Jake said with a tinge of melancholy. "He'd get me all hyped up about a fishing trip or a ball game or a day at the amusement park. Then something important at work would come up, and he'd cancel the trip."

"You said he cancelled out back then because he had important things to do. Did that make you feel unimportant and unwanted? Is that similar to how you feel now?"

"Yeah, that's a good way to describe it: unimportant and unwanted. Sometimes I feel like shaking him and asking, 'What's more important than your son, Dad?' But I know it wouldn't do any good."

"You feel like shaking him?" Marian probed gently. "Did that phone call today remind you how unimportant your dad made you feel? Is that why you got upset when you saw the garage door open?"

"Yes, I really feel ticked at my dad. Overlooking a young, insignificant boy who's always under foot is one thing. But I'm a man now, and he still doesn't think I'm worth very much. That hurts."

Uncovering Hidden Feelings

Jake is typical of countless numbers of men who explode at their wives and children, drive themselves to a heart attack, or overindulge in response to their anger. But with Marian's help, Jake is gradually leaving the ranks of men whose anger causes them to hurt themselves or others. He is learning to short-circuit destructive expressions of anger by identifying his feelings and resolving them in a positive way. Marian is a good example of how a wife can help her husband deal productively with angry feelings.

For most men, identifying, verbalizing, and dealing with feelings doesn't come easily. As we have already discussed, today's man grew up in a culture that taught him to hide his emotions behind a mask of confidence and machismo. This is the big-boys-don't-cry syndrome, and it has influenced virtually every man alive to some degree. Men have grown up emotionally underdeveloped and immature. They don't verbalize and deal with their feelings well because no one has taught them how to do it.

Choosing and Learning

It's not that men don't have feelings. They do, of course. They are affected emotionally when they aren't able to do something or when they can't change a situation they're in. They have feelings about responding to compliments and affection, hurt and rejection. They feel deeply when they perceive they are not valued by others as a worthwhile person. They feel jealousy, shame, guilt, helplessness, fear, disappointment, inferiority, depression, sadness, frustration, joy, loneliness, and inadequacy. And all these feelings boiling inside can contribute to his anger.

And it's not that men are incapable of being affective and expressive. That's the traditional view: men are men (rough and tumble, emotions well-controlled) and women are women (sugar and spice, emotions easily expressed). Rather, many contemporary sex role experts contend that

> individuals have the freedom to choose to incorporate positive characteristics into their behavior, regardless of whether they are considered stereotypically masculine or feminine attributes. . . . Androgynous [male and female characteristics in one] individuals are considered more well-rounded in the sense that they are not compelled to restrict their behaviors according to traditional sex role stereotypes.[1]

Don't be alarmed: By androgynous we're talking about men being free to break away from the masculine role stereotype in order to express and deal with their emotions in ways traditionally associated only with women. For example, traditional men don't cry, but androgynous men are free to cry because they know that tears are human, not male or female. Similarly, traditional men don't talk through their anger and resolve it with another person because they consider such behavior to be feminine. However, androgynous men are free to learn and practice this behavior because they know that its restriction to gender is no more than a myth.

When you ask a traditional man how he *feels*, he will usually tell you what he *thinks*. He doesn't know how to tell you about his feelings because such expression hasn't been part of his education or experience. But when you ask an androgynous man how he *feels*, he will tell you how he *feels*. He is able to do so for two reasons. First, he has chosen to bring his emotions to the surface. Second, someone helped him learn how to do it.

You may be thinking, "I want my husband to mature emotionally to the point that he can deal with his anger positively. Where can I find such a teacher?" The answer to your question is staring back at you whenever you look into a mirror: you! You are the most likely person to help your man develop this skill. First, you probably know him as intimately as anyone. He trusts you. He will respond to you. Second, you know about emotional expression because it hasn't been suppressed in females in our culture as it has been in males.

As you begin to help him in this area, remember: Behind his cool, confident facade hides a frightened little boy who is still searching for himself as a man. To him, beginning to deal with his emotions is like walking into a mine field. He's afraid that the next step forward may hurt him. He needs someone to guide him patiently through the mine field, someone to go with him and show him where to step.

Help Him Learn to Talk

When a woman's emotions come to the surface, she tends to want to talk about them and explain them. But when a man's emotions come into play in his life, he tends to want to fix them and push them back under the surface where they belong. For example, when a woman gets angry over something, she'll usually call a friend to talk about it. But when a man gets angry over something, he may make an angry gesture, or say something crude, and then stuff his anger away. Talking about it is usually not an option. It is vital to your man's health and safety that he learn how to verbalize his anger as women do instead of try to "fix" it.

It's not that men don't know how to talk. They do. Studies show that most men tend to dominate conversations in mixed groups, even when they are outnumbered by women. But when men talk, they talk about things — money, the weather, business deals, sports, hobbies, etc. — while women talk about personal issues — children, husbands, friends, feelings, etc. Men can talk about personal issues too. But they usually don't because they have learned from their fathers and other models of masculinity that such topics are "woman talk."

How can you help your husband break free of this harmful sex role stereotype and begin to talk about his angry feelings with you? It's not an easy task, especially if your man is deeply entrenched in the masculine myth of the strong, silent type. He will need learn an entirely new language: the language of feelings. Here are a few suggestions that may help.

Ask Questions

When Marian noticed that Jake was upset about his dad bailing out on their hunting trip, she asked, "How do you feel about the trip being cancelled?" For some men, a direct question like this one is enough. They are able to answer by taking a good look at themselves and identifying the emotions that are in play. Once they have verbalized their basic feelings they are better equipped to channel them into constructive rather than destructive responses.

Use the "how do you feel" question often, even when you don't see any visible signs of aggravation or upset. Remember: Men are well-practiced at hiding negative feelings under the camouflage of an "everything's okay" appearance. Asking about his feelings in potentially irritating situations *before* he shows signs of anger may save you and him a lot of grief. Here are some examples:

- How did you feel about your son sitting on the bench during most of his Little League game?
- How do you feel about spending Thanksgiving weekend at my mother's place?
- How do you feel about being passed over for the promotion?
- How did you feel about me taking the initiative in love-making last night?
- How do you feel about being tail-gated on the freeway?
- How did you feel when you learned that your daughter received only Cs and Ds on her report card this term?
- How do you feel when the TV goes on the fritz during your favorite program?
- How do you feel when your father spends more time with your sister and her children than he does with us?

Some men need more help in expressing their feelings than the simple question, "How do you feel?" They certainly know they're feeling something, and they may even be able to call it anger. But anger is such a general term that when they are pressed to be more specific about their feelings they draw a blank.

Be prepared to offer multiple choice answers when you ask about your husband's feelings. For example, Marian followed up her how-do-you-feel question by asking Jake, "Did that phone call today remind you how unimportant your dad made you feel?" Jake was angry because he felt unimportant, but Marian's gentle probing helped him bring his feelings into even clearer focus.

The list of synonyms you can suggest to help your husband verbalize his feelings is practically endless. Family counselor Norm Wright offers this list of synonyms in eight categories of feelings, including anger. You may want to use lists like these to help your husband pinpoint exactly what is going on inside him:

Hate	Fear	Anger	Happiness
1. dislike	fright	sore	joyful
2. bitter	terror	offended	enthusiastic
3. hateful	anxious	mad	merry
4. odious	misgivings	resentful	lucky
5. detest	concern	wrathful	fortunate
6. spiteful	harassed	hostile	pleased
7. aversion	dread	displeased	glad
8. despise	alarm	injured	satisfied
9. loathe	apprehension	vexed	contented
10. abominate	worry	torment	delighted

Love	Disappointment	Sadness	Confusion
1. affection	disturbed	fearful	mixed-up
2. loving	unhappy	grief	doubtful
3. amorous	dissatisfied	dejected	disorder
4. likable	frustrated	torment	bewilderment
5. tenderness	deluded	anguish	confounded
6. devotion	defeated	sorrow	disarray
7. attachment	hurt	unhappy	jumble
8. fondness	failure	gloomy	uncertain
9. passion	rejection	melancholy	perplexed
10. endearing	thwarted	mournful	embarrassment[2]

Notice in Jake and Marian's conversation that Marian referred to something Jake said that tipped her off about the source of his anger: "You said he cancelled out back then because he had important things to do. Did that make you feel unimportant and unwanted? Is that similar to how you feel now?" Listen for clues in what he says to help you ask the right kinds of questions.

Furthermore, whenever possible avoid questions that can be answered with a simple yes or no. And when you ask yes-or-no questions, be sure to add, "Why?" The goal is to have him talk about his anger not just acknowledge or deny it with a nod or a grunt. Frame your questions in order to encourage dialogue.

Show Interest in Him

Your inquisitiveness about his feelings will seem contrived, however, if you're only interested in talking to him when he seems ready to explode. Getting him to talk about his anger will be easier if he perceives that you are also interested in talking about other parts of his life. The more familiar you become with his activities and interests, especially those outside the home, the better prepared you will be to help him identify and talk about his anger.

Show interest in his job. Ask him frequently about the projects he's working on, the people he's working with, and the pressures he feels. If possible, visit him at his job site and meet his superiors, coworkers, and subordinates. As he becomes more comfortable talking with you about his work, he may find it easier to open up about the things that make him angry on the job.

Show interest in his hobbies. Ask him about his golf score, his hardest hole, his best shot of the day, etc. Volunteer to help him tie flies or to go with him on his next fishing trip. If he collects stamps, coins, bottles, etc., ask him what you should be watching for to help him enlarge his collection.

Show interest in his background. A man's anger is often rooted in his family history. How much do you know about his parents, brothers, sisters, grandparents, and other relatives? Ask him about his family background: how he felt about his parents and siblings as a child, how much his grandparents, aunts, and uncles were involved in raising him, what he would change about his childhood, etc. Suggest that the two of you put together a family photo album that traces the history of both families. Working on such a project is a perfect opportunity for you to ask questions like, "What kind of person was your grandfather?"

As we explained early in the book, a significant amount of a man's anger can be traced to his relationship — or more correctly, lack of relationship — with his father. So in order to deal thoroughly with his anger, eventually he will need to talk about his relationship with his dad — past and present. This is usually a tender spot with men, because so many of them feel like Jake: unimportant and unloved by their fathers. Don't push the issue. As you show genuine interest in his life, including his family background, you are preparing the soil for fruitful dialogue when the time is right.

Back Off and Listen

Someone has observed that God gave us two ears but only one mouth, which should tell us something about the proper ratio of listening to speaking in our relationships. In his book *Communication: Key to Your Marriage,* Norm Wright underscores the importance of listening in a husband-wife relationship:

> Listening effectively means that when someone is talking you are not thinking about what you are going to say when the other person stops. Instead, you are totally tuned in to what the other person is saying. . . . Real listening is receiving and accepting the message as it is sent — seeking to understand what the other person really means. When this happens you can go further than saying, "I hear you." You can say, "I hear what you mean." [3]

Unfortunately, we often reverse this emphasis, especially when trying to "help" a spouse or family member. You see his problem clearly, and you know you can help him if he will only shut-up and listen to you. You can't resist the urge to jump in and talk for him, finish his sentences, correct his observations, etc. But instead of opening up to healthy communication in this setting, often a man closes up under the pressure of being bombarded by "advice." Helping him learn to talk about his feelings means you will need to learn to back off and listen when he's ready to talk. You must resist the urge to talk for him. His conclusions may not always be as insightful as yours, but they will be more meaningful to him because they are his own. When you back off to a safe distance of questioning and listening, he will feel free to start talking.

The Pressure Is Off

Earlier in the chapter we left Jake and Marian in the middle of a conversation in their basement laundry room. They continued to talk about Jake's feelings of anger for several minutes. As Marian drew him out with non-threatening questions and comments, the conversation lifted a lot of hostility off Jake's chest. It was as if a pressure valve inside him had been slowly opened while they talked. Jake relaxed and sat down near Marian.

When the washer completed its cycle, Jake told Marian that he was going to talk to his father in the coming week about some of his feelings. He thanked her for helping him think through his feelings and avoid an angry outburst at Philip. They shared a brief prayer together. Then as Marian moved the clean laundry to the dryer, Jake went upstairs to ask Philip if he wanted to go duck hunting with him in the morning.

Jake's feelings of anger needed an outlet that day, and he had a number of negative options. He could have exploded at Marian or Philip in verbal or physical rage (he was well on his way when he charged through the front door). He could have headed off to the nearest tavern to drown his feelings in a sea of alcohol. He could have clammed up, locked himself in his little shop inside the garage, and allowed his anger to eat away at his insides. But, thanks to Marian, he was able to deal with his anger in a positive way.

There are two significant steps you can take to effect the same results in your angry man. These steps are suggested in a letter in the New Testament written by James. He writes:

"Confess your sins to each other and pray for each other so that you may be healed" (James 5:16). We're not saying that all anger is sin; it's not. But feelings of anger degenerate so quickly into hostile, sinful attitudes and actions that this verse often applies.

The first step is *confession*. To confess means to get it out in the open, verbalize it, identify it clearly for what it is. In a religious context, to confess also means to agree with God's view on a topic. God says that anger leading to hurtful words or deeds is wrong. When your man says, "I feel like punching that guy's lights out, but I know it would be a wrong response," he's confessing, he's agreeing with God that an angry attack is wrong.

The second step is *prayer*. God is the One who created your man's emotions, and He can help him control them. Just as our Lord quieted the stormy sea, He can quiet the hostile heart if we ask Him through prayer to do so. A woman who will pray for and with her husband concerning his anger will be a great help to him.

The result of confession and prayer is *healing* as men discover and live out a more positive masculine identity. Having confessed and prayed through his anger and other difficult emotions, a man is free to follow Christ's example of relationship, not remoteness. He can learn to give up his detachment from you, from his parents, and from his peers and live out his values, beliefs, and positive feelings.

Your husband can recover much of his true masculinity in the presence and caring of other men. What has been termed "the tear in the masculine soul" in a man began with his isolation from his father and other positive masculine models. It is healed when men share their lonely pilgrimages with each other, when they are transparent and real with each other, and when they join in nurturing, non-competitive friendships.

The church is an ideal place for this kind of nurturing and healing to take place. It's a place where men can come together in small support groups to get to know one another and can care for each other as men, sons, husbands, and fathers.

Destructive patterns of dealing with anger can be forgiven and corrected. Productive ways can be initiated. Your man's anger can find a positive, healthy outlet if you help him learn to talk to you and God about it before it goes out of control.

Think about It, Talk about It with Him

1. Is your husband more traditional or androgynous when it comes to dealing with his emotions? Mark an "X" on the line below at a point the represents where he is between the two extremes. The strictly traditional male is very closed about discussing his feelings, and the strictly androgynous male is very open about it.

Traditional _____ Androgynous
    Man   Man

2. How would you rate yourself at the skill of asking questions to draw your husband into discussing his anger?

Excellent Very Good   Good   Fair   Poor Very Poor   Awful

3. What one step could you take to improve your skill in this area?

4. How would you rate yourself at the skill of showing interest in him?

Excellent Very Good   Good   Fair   Poor Very Poor   Awful

5. What one step could you take to improve your skill in this area?

6. How would you rate yourself at the skill of backing off and listening when he talks?

Excellent   Very Good   Good   Fair   Poor   Very Poor   Awful

7. What one step could you take to improve your skill in this area?

8. How would you rate yourself at the skill of helping him confess and pray about his anger?

Excellent   Very Good   Good   Fair   Poor   Very Poor   Awful

9. What one step could you take to improve your skill in this area?

9

Learning to Relate

Experts in human behavior generally agree that men and women have the same basic psychological needs, including the need to be significantly involved in the lives of other people. We've all felt the sting of loneliness at some time in our lives. You spend several days in a distant city on business. You don't know a soul, so you travel, eat, and sleep alone. You may strike up a conversation with a stranger on an airplane or in a restaurant, but you miss your family and friends. You can't wait to get back home to those you love. Each of us is created to know, accept, and love others and to be known, accepted, and loved by others.

Experts also agree that, although his need is as great as a woman's, a man is generally less skillful and less comfortable in establishing and maintaining the loving, nurturing relationships he needs. The typical male is socially immature and insecure. He keeps most of his relationships at a distance because he's self-conscious about his underdeveloped social skills. When invited to the boss's party, his niece's wedding reception, or the next door neighbor's open house, he usually looks for an excuse to duck out early if he can't find a way to skip it altogether.

As we have already discussed, the social immaturity that is characteristic of our masculine population is a byproduct of the stereotyped sex roles that have emerged in our culture over the last 100 years. Deeply influenced by a hard-working father and an achievement-oriented culture, today's man believes that masculinity is equated with doing, earning, and succeeding, while being, relating, and conversing are feminine traits. Having adopted this mythical masculine sex role, today's man is in effect standing on his own air hose. In an effort to be a real man by society's standards, he shoves his relationships to the back burner. But in so doing he blocks the primary means by which his deep need for acceptance, love, and interdependence can be met. And his lack of social "oxygen" has made him angry.

If a man is going to find peace from his frustration and anger, he needs to learn how to relate effectively to others. Again, you are the prime candidate to help him. Being a woman, you have clearer insight and more experience in this area because relationships are your strong suit.

Levels of Intimacy in Relationship

How can you help your husband begin to relate to others in a way that will meet his relational needs and the needs of others? The answer is "very slowly." A deep-sea diver must ascend slowly from the ocean floor to the surface of the water to allow his body time to adjust to the change in atmospheric pressure. If he rises too rapidly nitrogen bubbles will form in his blood and body tissue causing tightness in the chest, pains in the joints, and convulsions and collapse in severe cases. Similarly, if you try to move your husband too rapidly from where he is to where he should be in his relationships, he may become too uncomfortable and retreat.

Relationships begin with people purposely spending time together. You may object, "My man and I spend time together all right, but I wouldn't call what we have a relationship. We eat at the same table, watch TV in the same family room, and sleep in the same bed, but he hardly says a word. I talk and he nods or grunts. If time spent together is the basis of a relationship, my dog and I relate better." You may have a similar objection regarding your man and his children, his poker buddies, or his coworkers. They may spend time together, but how they interact doesn't come close to resembling an intimate loving, nurturing relationship.

Agreed: Time spent together is only a beginning, the lowest common denominator. Relating to another person involves much more than being in the same room. But you've got to start somewhere. In order for people to relate to one another in a meaningful way, they must converse with each other as they spend time together.

In his book for couples, *Romancing Your Marriage*, Norm Wright identifies five levels of conversation corresponding to five levels of intimacy in a relationship. Since the typical male in our culture is socially immature, your husband may only be experienced and confident at the lower, less threatening levels of communication and intimacy. Yet many of his deepest relational needs can only be met as he experiences deeper levels of intimacy with you and other significant people in his life. Here is a quick summary of the five levels of conversation and intimacy. [1]

Level 1: Sharing general facts and information. Conversation at this level is not much deeper than talking about the news, sports, and weather. You're basically exchanging news about people, things, and events without sharing ideas or opinions. Level 1 conversation is strictly from the head.

Level 2: Sharing the ideas and opinions of others. Here you're only a little deeper than at Level 1. You're reporting opinions and feelings about the information you exchange, but they are the opinions and feelings of others, not your own. Conversation is still almost entirely from the head.

Level 3: Sharing your own ideas and opinions. At this level you are approaching moderate intimacy. You are risking minor vulnerability by disclosing some of your own ideas and opinions, but you are still not revealing who you really are. You're beginning to talk from the heart, but most of what you say is still from the head.

Level 4: Sharing your own preferences, beliefs, concerns, and experiences. Level 4 conversation involves a high degree of intimacy as you speak freely of your past and present involvement with the topic. At this point you are talking more from the heart than from the head, but you still hold a portion of yourself in reserve.

Level 5: Sharing your inner feelings, likes, and dislikes. At this level you are completely transparent and vulnerable. You are open to talk about how people, things, and events touch you emotionally. You are now talking almost exclusively from the heart.

It is at these deeper levels of conversation and intimacy that a man's deep need for love, acceptance, and relationship can be fully met. The problem is that he is more comfortable sharing from his head than from his heart. He may perceive vulnerability to intimacy in conversation too great a risk to the macho image he feels he must maintain. Yet by holding others at arm's distance he feels frustrated, incomplete, and angry because his deepest relational needs are not being met.

Let's consider some practical ways you can lovingly encourage your husband to move from surface levels of intimacy to deeper levels.

Help Him Relate to You

The relationship which has the greatest opportunity to impact your husband's relational growth, of course, is his relationship with you. It's likely that he's closer to you than to anyone else. He already shares a high degree of physical and emotional intimacy with you. However, this doesn't necessarily mean that he bares his soul to you. Rather, if he's a typical male, he probably keeps much of his emotional and spiritual self safely locked behind closed doors, because the masculine code of behavior regards openness as a sign of weakness. But if there's anyone who has a chance of gaining access to his inner feelings, it's you.

What's the key to unlocking the doors to his deepest personal thoughts and feelings? What will move him from being a frightened, protective little boy to a vulnerable man willing to give to you as well as receive from you emotional intimacy? Your patient, probing questions. Without bugging him, nagging him, or pestering him, you can ask strategic questions that can unlock deeper levels of intimacy between you and deepen your relationship. And a man who enjoys an intimate, emotional relationship with his wife is well on his way to finding peace from his masculine anger.

Perhaps the best way to illustrate the use of questions is with a dialogue between a wife and her husband. In the following scenario, Reuben is meeting his wife Emily at a restaurant for lunch during their respective lunch hours. Reuben is in turmoil because he has just learned that the large company he works for will by laying off several hundred employees in two weeks. Reuben is suspicious that his division will be subject to some of the deepest cuts and that his position may not survive.

Notice that Emily begins her questions at Level 1 and gradually progresses to deeper levels of intimacy. For the sake of our illustration, Reuben will answer all of Emily's questions honestly, even to Level 5. In reality, if your man balks at a certain level on a topic, don't push him. It may take several conversations over a period of months for him to feel comfortable moving into a new level of intimacy. If you demand that he answer when he is uncomfortable at that level you will only retard his relational growth and increase his anger.

REUBEN: I'm sure glad we could get together for lunch today, Emily. I've had a pretty rough morning. It looks like a massive layoff is only two weeks away.

EMILY: Who gave the announcement? What did they say? (Level 1: General facts and information).

REUBEN: Mr. Jackson, the executive vice president, told us in a meeting of department heads this morning. He said that the cuts are pretty deep and that some departments may be completely eliminated. He said they are especially looking at the marketing division.

EMILY: That's your division, Reuben. They could be thinking about eliminating your telemarketing department. That would mean 15 people losing their jobs, including you.

REUBEN: Right.

EMILY: What do some of the other department heads think is going to happen? (Level 2: Ideas and opinions of others).

REUBEN: Sal, my boss, thinks that telemarketing is definitely on the chopping block. He says our numbers look pretty good but that we are expendable compared to other marketing departments. Everybody I talked to felt that if the department goes, I go — either into another department or out the door completely.

EMILY: What do you think is going to happen? What are some options if your department is axed? (Level 3: Reuben's ideas and opinions).

REUBEN: From all I've heard, I don't think my department will make it. It seems only logical to me for them to cut the department that contributes the least. As for me, Jackson may offer me a management position in sales since that's the division I came from. But there will obviously be some cuts there, and they may not have a spot for me. My gut feeling is that I will be looking for a job in two weeks.

EMILY: What would you rather do: stay with the company in some capacity or start over with another organization? (Level 4: Reuben's preferences and concerns).

REUBEN: My first choice would be to stay where I'm at. We're just starting to make some headway in telemarketing, and I think the company would make a big mistake by dropping the whole program. I'd like to convince Jackson to keep me and two of my phone people. That would be a significant cut, but we would still be a viable department. If it came to a choice between moving to another department and leaving the company, I think I'd opt to leave and look for another place to practice what I've learned about telemarketing.

EMILY: How do you feel about the prospect of being out of a job? (Level 5: Reuben's inner feelings, likes, and dislikes).

REUBEN: The first thing to hit me was fear. Even if I catch on with another company right away I probably won't earn as much, and that's going to hurt us financially. And what if I can't find another job right away? With all the bills we have, that thought terrifies me. Then I started feeling angry. I kept thinking about all the time and energy I've invested in the telemarketing department going up in smoke. What a waste, especially when we are doing so well!

These five levels of questions can also be used to encourage emotional transparency in a man on more personal issues. For many men, their relationship with their father is a primary source of unresolved anger. In the following scene, Craig and his fiancee, Kelly, are returning from a visit with Craig's father in the hospital after his heart by-pass operation. Kelly uses the opportunity to gently probe Craig about his relationship with his father.

KELLY: Tell me about your father, Craig. What kind of work did he do before I knew him? Was he in a high-stress profession that contributed to his heart condition? (Level 1: General facts and information)

CRAIG: Dad used to be a minister. But about six years ago he left the ministry and became the funeral director at the mortuary in town. He's had a lot of stress in both jobs. As a minister he felt responsible for the entire congregation, and he worked day and night trying to meet their spiritual needs. And at the funeral home he took each family's grief personally. He went out of his way to comfort them and tailor the funeral to meet their needs. All those hours must have caught up with him.

KELLY: How did your family feel about your dad spending so much time away from home? (Level 2: Sharing the ideas and opinions of others)

CRAIG: When my older sisters and I were small, Mom tolerated Dad being out several nights a week for meetings and visitation. She felt that he was doing God's will. As we got older, Mom even went with him more often, leaving me in the care of my oldest sister. The girls didn't mind our parents being gone in the evenings because they got to do whatever they wanted. By the time Dad switched to the funeral home, Beth was married, Ruth was in college, and I was in high school. Dad was still out several nights a week comforting the bereaved, but Mom couldn't keep up the pace, so she stayed home with me. And she wasn't happy about being left out of Dad's business affairs.

KELLY: It must have been hard to grow up without your dad around much of the time. What did you think about his job and all the time it demanded from him? (Level 3: Craig's ideas and opinions)

CRAIG: I understood that ministers and funeral directors didn't have 8-to-5 type jobs. But I thought it was wrong for Dad and Mom to spend more time taking care of other people and their children than they spent on us. I thought that if Dad were out three or four nights a week he could at least spend Saturday or Sunday afternoon with his kids. But I realized that those were good days to catch people at home, so he was often gone then too. When Dad left the church, there were a lot of rumors flying around that the Board canned him because he had been intimate with some of the women he regularly visited.

KELLY: Do you think he was guilty of impropriety? (Level 4: Craig's preferences, beliefs, concerns, and experiences)

CRAIG: It's hard not to believe it. The Board must have had some tangible evidence; they couldn't just can him on hearsay. And knowing some of the women he visited, I think he probably did get involved a time or two. But I'm concerned that he never leveled with my mother, my sisters, or me about it. It's typical of him to run away from his problems instead of face them. No wonder his ticker gave out.

KELLY: How do you feel about your father not being closer to his family and possibly dragging the family name through the mud with his misbehavior? (Level 5: Craig's inner feelings, likes, and dislikes)

CRAIG: First, I'm angry at Dad and Mom for abandoning me to my sisters all those nights and weekends while they were out doing "God's work." Second, I'm angry at Dad for not talking to me about the allegations of misconduct against him. If he's guilty, fine; I can forgive him. And if he's innocent, I'd just like to know. But he has avoided this issue just like everything else, and I'm just fed up with him.

Remember: It's unlikely that you will be able to lead him through all five levels of conversation and intimacy on a topic in one sitting. It may take several conversations and much patience to get to a Level 5 dimension on topics that he closely guards. That's okay. It's better to back off and count time as your ally than to charge ahead and complicate his difficulty with expressing his deepest feelings. As you patiently question him and model openness and transparency yourself, he will learn to relate to you in ways that will bring him peace.

Help Him Relate to Others

It won't be quite as easy for you to help your husband with his other relationships. In fact, if you're not careful, anything you do to encourage him to relate to others may be interpreted by him or them as meddling. So you would be wise to keep a low profile to avoid mothering or nagging. Instead, watch for timely opportunities to offer positive ideas for improving your man's relationships on the following levels.

Relating to His Children

If you, your husband, and your children constitute a nuclear family living under the same roof, there are many ways you can help implement healthy interaction between a father and his kids. Each of the following ideas opens the door for him and your children to meet each other's deepest relational needs.

Include kids in parental discussions. There are occasions when it is appropriate for your children to take part in serious conversations between Mom and Dad. For example, Reuben and Emily's nine-year-old daughter, Katy, may benefit from listening to her parents talk at all five levels of conversation and intimacy about Reuben's impending layoff. Katy may gain tremendous insight into her father's feelings as she listens to him describe his fears about finding another job. Reuben may also discover that Katy is a ready source of emotional support as she promises to pray for him and encourage him through the process of the layoff and job search.

Of course, there are some topics of parental conversation that are inappropriate for children. But there are many other occasions when parents and children can grow closer in relationship by talking through a topic at all five levels of intimacy. Watch for those opportunities, and then suggest to your man, "It might be healthy to have the kids in on this discussion. Would that be okay with you?"

Promote family discussions at home. From time to time, suggest that the kids and their father turn off the TV and gather around the kitchen table with you to play games. (Prepare some popcorn or cookies to help lure them and keep them in the kitchen!) As you play a table game, introduce light topics of conversation that will get the children talking with their father. For example, you might say, "Honey, what kinds of games did you play when you were a child? How did you feel when you won? When you lost? Did your parents play games with you? What did your parents talk about with you?" etc. Hopefully your children will feel free to also ask questions which will draw their father into deeper levels of conversation.

Many discussions can take place around the family photo album. Sit down with the album occasionally and talk about the events represented by the photos. Prompt the children to ask their father about his life as a teenager, the jobs he has held, his years in the armed forces, etc. Each picture in the album has the potential for helping your children get to know their father better.

Promote traveling discussions. Your husband and your children are a captive audience when they are traveling with you in the car. When it's appropriate, suggest that you play simple conversation games that will get father and children (and you too) talking together. For example, play the game "Feelings." Give each person the opportunity to ask every one else in the car a question about feelings, like, "When were you very afraid?" After both parents and each child has answered, someone else can ask another question about feelings, such as, "What was the happiest day of your life?" As fathers and children learn to verbalize their feelings to each other as easily as they talk about what's for dinner, the emotional bond between them will deepen.

Relating to His Parents

If your husband's father and/or mother are still alive, you can be a gentle instrument of encouragement for a positive relationship between them. In many families, communication between a man and his parents is often relayed through his wife. If your family is typical, you tell your mother-in-law by phone or mail about all the news in your family, and she tells you all the news about her end of the family, which you condense to a sentence and relay to your husband. Here are several ways to encourage him to improve his relationship with his parents.

Encourage personal correspondence. If his parents live a great distance away, try to involve him in your correspondence with them. When they write, volunteer to read the letter to him aloud (he may not read it himself even if you leave it on his night stand!). When you write to them, say to your husband, "I'm jotting a note to your Mom and Dad. Would you like to add a paragraph or two before I close?" He may agree to writing a couple of paragraphs where he wouldn't be willing to write an entire letter by himself.

Similarly, when you talk to your in-laws by telephone, invite your husband to come on the line for a few minutes "just to say hello." He may be willing to participate in "your" conversation where he would not initiate a call himself.

Encourage personal visits. If his parents are close enough to visit regularly, take the initiative for getting together with them by inviting them over for dinner, family birthday celebrations, holidays, etc. When he and his parents are together, employ some of the same conversation strategies you use with your children. Use the family albums, slides, or home movies to prompt discussions of family activities in the past. Follow the five levels of conversational intimacy described earlier to help move family conversations from a surface level to a meaningful exchange of opinions and feelings. Look for subtle opportunities to help him and his parents communicate at deeper levels. The better he feels about his relationship with them, the more he will be at peace with himself and with you.

Relating to His Friends

Roscoe and Arnie were friends for 45 years. They met while working together for the Department of Water and Power in a large city. Before they retired, they played golf together every Saturday, and they got together with a few other guys from the yard on Tuesday nights for poker. When Roscoe and Arnie retired within four months of each other, they started playing golf three times a week. And Roscoe, Arnie, and their wives got into the habit of going out to dinner together on each other's birthdays. They gradually lost touch with their other friends from the Department.

When Roscoe was diagnosed with colon cancer, he bravely endured chemotherapy and two surgeries before he passed away at age 68. After the funeral, the minister, who knew both men only casually, said to Arnie, "You men have been close friends for two-thirds of your lives. Roscoe must have confided in you about his hope for recovery, his fear of dying, and his remorse at leaving Estelle behind." "Nope, Reverend," Arnie replied, wiping the tears from his eyes. "We talked about golf, fishing, poker, and underground conduit. We *didn't* talk about what we were afraid of. We were good friends, Reverend, but we weren't brothers." Unfortunately, many men view their friendships with other men the way Roscoe and Arnie viewed theirs. For them, a friend is someone to enjoy working with, going fishing with, playing golf with, or racing stock cars with. But the relationship rarely gets much deeper than what they do together. The macho code of mythical masculinity prevents them from revealing their fears, dreams, weaknesses, mistakes, or hurts to each other.

Today's man would probably do better at handling the stresses of job and family if he had some friends who were more like brothers: men to whom he could bare his soul and still be completely accepted. If your husband doesn't have such a friend, you may be able to provide an atmosphere for his relationship to deepen with the men he calls his friends.

Offer to invite his friends — along with their wives or girl friends — over for dinner occasionally. When it's appropriate during the conversation, inject questions from Levels 3, 4, and 5. For example, as a man is describing his work to you, ask questions like, "What's the most dangerous or risky part of what you do? What kinds of people are the hardest for you to get along with in your work? What do you think you'd be doing if you didn't have this job? Are you afraid that you will be fired or laid off? What would you do if you lost your job?"

Do your part to enlarge his circle of friends. With his full agreement, invite new couples in the neighborhood or at church over to dinner. Plan a dinner or an outing with your girl friends and include their husbands. And always allow plenty of time in the activity for the men to get together and talk.

Relating to a Mentor

As cited earlier in this book, most men today report that they don't (or didn't) have a good relationship with their fathers. The cultural pressure on men to regard career above family has left many adult sons without mentors for masculinity. Men today are angry because their fathers didn't teach them or model for them what it means to be a man.

If your husband was not mentored by his father, he may still be subconsciously looking for a father figure to take him under his wing and show him what it means to be a real man. He especially needs to learn from a father/mentor what it means to be a man emotionally. If the opportunity arises, talk to your man about the benefits of having a father-mentor figure to talk to and learn from.

Relating to God

Your husband's relationship with God, of course, is personal. It need not conform to your ideals of Christianity, religiosity, or spirituality. Perhaps the most effective way for you to encourage your man's relationship to God is to appreciate the godliness you already see in him. Tell him how thankful you are when he takes the lead in the spiritual matters of the home (e.g., helping the children get ready for church, leading family prayer and Bible study instead of waiting for you to do it, etc.).

You can further encourage these traits by asking him to pray for you each day and when you have a special need. For example, ask him to pray for you before going to work or at bedtime. Perhaps you face a decision at work that must be made within 30 minutes. Call him at work and ask him to pray over the phone, even if he prays silently, that God would give you direction for the decision. Then thank him for his willingness to be your spiritual partner, and keep him informed of the results of his prayer.

As you strive to be of assistance in enriching the relationships in your husband's life, continue to avoid the temptation to act like a mother forcing a spoonful of castor oil. You are not his mother. You are his partner, his friend, his equal. As long as you see yourself as such, and treat him as such, your efforts to encourage him in his relationships will be generally fruitful.

Think about It, Talk about It with Him

1. What percentage of your conversation with your husband occurs at each of the five levels of intimacy described in this chapter?

Level 1: Sharing general facts and information

0% 10% 20% 30% 40% 50% 60% 70% 80% 90% 100%

Level 2: Sharing the ideas and opinions of others.

0% 10% 20% 30% 40% 50% 60% 70% 80% 90% 100%

Level 3: Sharing your own ideas and opinions.

0% 10% 20% 30% 40% 50% 60% 70% 80% 90% 100%

Level 4: Sharing your own preferences, beliefs, concerns, and experiences.

0% 10% 20% 30% 40% 50% 60% 70% 80% 90% 100%

Level 5: Sharing your own inner feelings, likes, and dislikes.

0% 10% 20% 30% 40% 50% 60% 70% 80% 90% 100%

2. Based on your evaluation above of your interaction with your husband, what are three practical steps you could take to help improve your relationship with him?

a.

b.

c.

3. How would you rate his relationship with your children?

Excellent Very Good Good Fair Poor Very Poor Awful

4. What one suggestion from this chapter will you put into practice to help improve his relationship with your children?

5. How would you rate his relationship with his parents?

Excellent Very Good Good Fair Poor Very Poor Awful

6. What one suggestion from this chapter will you put into practice to help improve his relationship with his parents?

7. How would you rate his relationship with his friends?

Excellent Very Good Good Fair Poor Very Poor Awful

8. What one suggestion from this chapter will you put into practice to help improve his relationship with his friends?

9. Does he have an older man who serves as a mentor in his life? If so, who is he? If not, what opportunity do you have to suggest that he find a mentor?

10

Dealing with His Losses

I really don't know what's wrong with me," said 42-year-old Tyrone as he sat down with the counselor. "I've attained many of my personal and business goals. But I'm still breeding ulcers trying to climb higher up the ladder. With all my success, I'm still bummed out when someone else beats me to a big sale or a new account. I have a wonderful wife and two great kids, but I kind of feel like an outsider when I'm with them. I have lots of friends, and I'm around people all the time. But I don't enjoy it, and I don't think they really enjoy being with me. I'm afraid my dark moods are distancing me from the ones I love. But I don't know what to do about it."

Tyrone looks and acts like the American Dream personified. By all outward appearances he has succeeded in the areas of life that really matter in our society: family, friends, career, finances. But like so many men, Tyrone's warm smile and confident exterior mask a deep sadness and uncertainty. He often wonders what's really worthwhile in life. Despite all the trophies he has accumulated indicating that he's living life as a winner, Tyrone always feels like he's going down to defeat.

Alarmingly, psychologists and counselors are discovering that Tyrone's symptoms are the rule rather than the exception in the men they see. No matter how much success they enjoy, most men feel like losers. It's likely that the anger you perceive in your husband has its roots in a deep-seated sense that the losses in his life outweigh his gains.

Torn Up over His Losses

Catholic priest Ted Dobson aptly describes this condition as "the tear in the masculine soul." It's the deep spiritual and psychological wound at the center of a man's identity. The primary cause of this inner tear is the tremendous loss he feels, specifically the loss of his father. No matter what else he finds, acquires, or achieves in life, nothing seems to make up for the sense of deficit he brings into manhood from the lack of affirmation and validation of a father.

Men are the victims of other losses in life that tend to salt the inner wound. In the fiercely competitive business world, a man may experience losses at various levels every week: losing a contract to a competitor, failing to meet a production schedule, being overlooked for a raise or promotion, etc. As he progresses through life, he may become aware that his lifetime dream of being promoted to foreman, setting company sales records, starting his own business, or owning a BMW is lost to inability or lack of opportunity.

Approaching mid-life, he struggles with the reality that he is losing his physical speed, strength, and agility as well as his trim physique, excellent health, and hair. As his children reach adulthood he loses them to their own spouses or careers. And with the advancing years he loses his friends and perhaps his wife to death. Each new loss stings the man who has been conditioned to control his own destiny and win at all costs.

But the greatest pain for most men is the tear that results from growing up without the emotional support and encouragement of a father. This pain is deeper and more acute because it begins very early in the man's life and affects all his other endeavors and relationships.

Psychologist Joseph Venema relates that he has run into the difficulties created by the tear in the masculine soul. Venema states that these problems usually show up in three roles that men try to live out: the solitary role, the detached role, and the success-machine role.[1]

The Solitary Role

Evan owns a small machine shop which he operates with one employee. He prides himself on his precision craftsmanship that keeps a steady stream of customers lined up for months. He has been urged by many of them to expand his shop and hire more employees. But Evan likes things small and controllable. He likes being needed. He doesn't want to grow because he doesn't want to get in a position where he needs his customers more than they need him.

Evan has the same attitude about his relationship with his wife. He keeps his thoughts and feelings well hidden because he feels he must act as if he doesn't need anything from her. His wife and children don't feel that they know Evan because he never shares anything from his heart. He has no close friends.

Evan has learned from his culture that it's not manly to need anyone. He picked up early in life that his father obviously didn't need him. And by spending more time on his career than with his family, Evan's father conveyed the idea that Evan shouldn't need him either. So Evan grew up feeling that he must face life without any help.

Like Evan, many men with a tear in the masculine soul learn to live solitary lives. They feel that it's okay to be needed by others, but they cannot commit themselves to need anyone else. And yet their choice for solitude and distance flies in the face of their basic psychological needs for love, relationship, and intimacy. The longer the man plays the solitary role, the greater his sense of loss as he alienates himself from others. He's shutting others out just like his father shut him out.

The Detached Role

Tom is a clerk in a hectic government office. In the midst of all the daily pressures, Tom is regarded as one of the most even-tempered workers in the department. He's quiet and efficient, and he never seems to get riled at the impatient co-workers or tax-payers who call or visit his office.

Tom spends a lot of energy riding herd on his emotions because he feels that they are his enemy. Deep inside he believes that his father didn't like him as a boy because he was too much of a cry-baby and a "'fraidy-cat." Since he perceives that he lost his father by being too much of a sissy, Tom isn't about to further jeopardize his wounded soul by exposing his emotions as an adult. When he momentarily loses control, he is embarrassed because he doesn't know how to interpret his emotions or respond to them. So he continues to distance himself from his coworkers to avoid those uncomfortable situations.

His controlled emotional detachment also keeps him aloof from his wife. In the past, whenever Tom showed any signs of being troubled, angry, or fearful, she would ask him what was wrong. But his usual response was a curt "Nothing!" So she has learned not to ask.

Venema suggests that the man playing the detached role faces a loss even greater than the loss of his father: the control of his life. "He finds it difficult to live out the values he professes because he ignores his heart, the center from which his values come. As a result, a man with a masculine tear is often controlled by people and forces outside himself. Often he is addicted to work, money, football, alcohol, or drugs."[2]

Like Tom, many men tend to suffer their losses alone. They stuff their sense of defeat inside, thinking that a real man should be able to "take it." Yet as they continue to clamp down on the

fear and anger they feel at being abandoned, they tend to isolate themselves emotionally from the very ones they should
trust. Eventually they become emotionally frozen. They are so
dead inside that they have little to give to a relationship.
Countless numbers of wives endure frustrating relationships
with detached men who are emotionally dead because they
have insisted on suffering their losses alone.

The Success-Machine Role

A man who has lost his father struggles with the deep
and often unacknowledged fear that he is not manly enough.
After all, the main man in his life wasn't close enough to affirm
his masculinity, leaving a haunting doubt. So he combats his
sense of inadequacy by excelling in the arenas of competition,
work, and money. He must win, he must succeed to prove
himself. So he pursues work and success with the single-
mindedness of a machine. He would rather die than be thought
a coward or a quitter. Even small failures are deeply disturbing to him.

This is the role Tyrone is playing—working hard,
succeeding, but still feeling unfulfilled. He carries the nagging
suspicion that he hasn't done enough or earned enough to
prove to himself that he is a real man. So he drives himself
harder, puts in more hours, and keeps reaching for higher rungs
on the corporate ladder.

Yet trying to assuage his sense of loss by driving himself
to success is counter-productive. Tyrone's life is becoming
lopsided. Vital interests and priorities such as family, personal
health, and spiritual life are taking a back seat. While working
to prove that he is worthy of love, he ends up damaging or
destroying relationships with those who already love him,
deepening the tear in his masculine soul.

Men who adopt the solitary role, the detached role, or the
success-machine role soon become angry men. Why? Because
the roles they play block them from experiencing and expressing their true masculinity.

Turning a Man's Losses into Gains

Until two years ago, 44-year-old Burt would have found it difficult to believe that his life would amount to anything but a total loss. It took a patient, loving Christian wife to help him come to terms with a life of rejection, abuse, violence, crime, and alcoholism.

Burt and his four brothers were born to a loving mother and a drunken, violent father whom they learned early to fear. When the boys were very young their mother fled from her abusive husband, giving up her four sons to foster care. Burt grew up in a number of foster homes, many unloving and some even abusive. He was frequently told that his real father and mother abandoned him because he was no good. As a young teen he tried to escape his inner pain by experimenting with drugs and alcohol. He never finished high school.

At age 18 Burt joined the Navy, but he wasn't emotionally equipped for his new-found freedom. He launched into a life of drinking, violence, and crime that eventually earned him a dishonorable discharge. Returning home, Burt's life was out of control, but he didn't care. He seemed destined to destroy everything in his path. He was arrested for burglary and spent three months in jail. Two days after he was released Burt was arrested again for attempted robbery and assaulting a police officer. He was sentenced to two years in prison.

The next 15 years of Burt's life comprised a downward spiral of substance abuse, failed jobs, crime, and prison. The one bright spot was his courtship and marriage to a girl he met during a brief period of sobriety. But within months of their wedding he "fell off the wagon" again and got in trouble with the law. While he was in prison his bride filed for divorce.

Feeling emotionally destitute over his lost life, Burt called for the prison chaplain. The chaplain urged Burt to give his life to God and start living by the principles in the Bible. Nothing else he had tried had worked so far, so Burt prayed a feeble prayer and asked God to make something of his life.

Within the year Burt was released to the care of a Christian half-way house where he began to learn about living for God on a daily basis. As he worked on his recovery, Burt found a decent job and moved out on his own.

Two years later he met Bea, a wonderful Christian widow. Bea knew that Burt had a long way to go before he was at peace with the hurt, loss, and anger that had characterized the first 40 years of his life. But she also saw how far he had come in his recovery. Burt and Bea were married after a six-month courtship.

Today the couple has a two-year-old son and a healthy, positive, growing relationship. They both have worked hard on helping Burt deal with his past and finding healing for the tear in his soul.

It's not likely that the pain and loss in your husband's past reached the proportions experienced by Burt. But it *is* likely that his soul has been torn to some degree by the loss of his father as well as by other losses he has suffered. Your role can be just as important as Bea's was in Burt's recovery. Here are some guidelines to assist you in this task.

Growing through Pain

One of the reasons that Bea was so instrumental in Burt's recovery from his past was her attitude toward all that had happened in his life. She didn't see Burt's losses as liabilities to his growth; she saw them as assets. She refused to accept the rejection, abuse, and pain he had suffered as handicaps; she treated them as stepping stones to his growth.

The first step to helping any man deal with his losses is to alert him to the positive role pain plays in personal growth. People who don't experience pain and loss don't experience much personal or emotional growth. When life is too easy, we don't grow. You can help your husband see that he is not penalized for life by the negative experiences in his past. Every painful experience — rejection by his father, a failed business, a disability of some kind — is an opportunity for growth. He must learn to accept them and use them as stepping stones to move ahead in the present.

Burt was initially drawn to Bea by her positive attitude about him. He confided in a counselor shortly after they were married, "I was afraid at first to tell her where I had come from and everything I had done. I was so embarrassed. I knew God had forgiven me, but I really hadn't forgiven myself. In fact, I was kind of scared that my past was somehow going to ruin my future with her.

"But as we got better acquainted I finally told her about my upbringing — the abuse by my father, the split-up of the family. I rather expected her to back off at that point, but she kept asking about me so I kept talking. I told her that I was a recovering alcoholic, then told her about my long and sordid history with the law. I wouldn't have blamed Bea for calling off our relationship after hearing all the gruesome details. But she was actually excited. She talked about God's grace in turning my losses into gains. She said I shouldn't be ashamed about what happened to me, because God was going to transform those minuses into pluses. The more I realized how deeply she really believed that, the more I began to believe it. It's been incredible!"

There's no way you can convince your husband of the growth potential in his pain if you don't believe it yourself, of course. But as you learn to view his losses from God's perspective, you will be able to help him see them as opportunities God has allowed for him to grow emotionally.

Talking about His Losses

The Bible instructs us to "carry each other's burdens" (Galatians 6:2). A vital part of any love relationship is the commitment each partner makes to help the other endure and survive times of trouble. The growth that comes through pain is only experienced as we share our pain with someone else.

In your relationship, you can fulfill your burden-bearing commitment by helping him carry the weight of the losses that have wounded his masculine soul.

But it will be difficult for you to help him carry his burdens if he doesn't tell you what they are. You can't very well help him grow through the pain of his losses if he won't verbalize them to you. And, as already discussed, most men don't readily talk about their hurts and losses. Men are more prone to handle pain and loss personally and internally, not relationally and verbally.

A primary means for helping your husband deal with his losses is getting him to talk about them. It may take him a while to do so, but ultimately he needs to talk with you, even about his father. It's likely that he is carrying a certain degree of pain and sense of loss over his relationship with his father. He may be carrying inner scars from neglect, rejection, or abuse that have been hidden for years, even decades. He will remain an angry man until he brings his pain to the surface by talking about it. As you interact with him, you can help bear his burden.

The five levels of communication and intimacy described in the previous chapter provide an excellent pattern for drawing out a man's thoughts and feelings about his father. For example, had Bea employed this pattern with Burt during their courtship, their conversation might have sounded like this:

> *BEA:* We've known each other for quite a while now, but I still don't know much about your family. Tell me about your father. Was he tall and slender like you? Do you have the same color eyes and hair? What kind of work did he do?
> (Level 1: General facts and information).
>
> *BURT:* Actually he was rather short and stocky. I guess my build comes from my mother's side of the

family. My resemblance to my dad is in my facial features—close-set eyes, narrow nose, small mouth. As for his occupation, he was a steelworker.

BEA: Did he have a lot of friends? Was he well-liked? What did others think of him?
(Level 2: Ideas and opinions of others).

BURT: The men Dad ran around with at the steel mill were pretty close, at least as close as rough, tough steel men get. They worked together and drank together. Anybody from the outside who threatened any one of them had to take on the bunch of them. Dad was one of the roughest of the bunch. I'm sure Mom was attracted to him at first by his macho image. But the more he drank, the more violent he became. Mom grew to hate him for the things he did to her and to her sons.

BEA: What do you think of him as a husband to your mother and as a father?
(Level 3: Burt's ideas and opinions).

BURT: To be honest, I don't know a man who is a worse example of a husband and father. When Dad wasn't working he was either drunk, getting drunk, or hung over. He beat Mom and he beat the four of us—when he could find us or catch us. We were so afraid of him that we got pretty good at hiding out until he drank himself to sleep.

BEA: Why do you think your dad was such a violent and hurtful husband and father? Do you think he'll ever change?
(Level 4: Burt's preferences, beliefs, concerns, and experiences).

BURT: I guess he had a pretty sad childhood himself. He was abandoned by his father and fell in with a very rough crowd. He started drinking at a younger age than I did. But that's no excuse for him to treat Mom and us like he did. I turned my life around, why couldn't he? God has His hands full with my dad. I don't think he'll ever change, and I'm not planning to have anything to do with him until he does.

BEA: How would you describe your deepest feelings for your dad? Do you feel any love at all? Do you ever feel sorry for him?
(Level 5: Burt's feelings, likes, and dislikes).

BURT: I've had a hard time with my feelings for Dad. Before I became a Christian I despised him. He caused a great deal of hurt in me and the people I love, and I could only wish him hurt in return. Love or pity for Dad? If I had any of those feelings they were buried under a mountain of hurt and hatred. When God came into my life I expected all those ugly feelings to go away. But I've struggled with them. I've tried to forgive my dad, but it's been hard. God has given me a love for my dad, and someday soon I need to go see him and make things right.

Remember: You probably won't be able to talk your husband through the five levels of conversation and intimacy as quickly and successfully as in this fictionalized example. This is only an example of the five levels and how they work. It may take you weeks to win enough of his trust to move him into sharing the deeper levels of his personal feelings. But as you continue to love him and accept his past and his losses, he will eventually feel comfortable about sharing his burden with you.

Learning to Listen

Getting a man to talk about his losses is only half the battle. In order for you to really share his burden you must learn to listen to what he says. This isn't always as easy as it may sound. He may stumble over his words and fail to explain himself clearly. He may make light of his losses because it embarrasses him to talk about them. He may avoid a lot of important detail because he just doesn't think it's important. In short, you may find it difficult to listen to him.

As he struggles to put his feelings into words, you will be tempted to jump in and talk for him. Don't do it! The importance of listening to him patiently even when he struggles to communicate cannot be overemphasized. He must tell his story at his own pace and in his own words. As Norm Wright cautions,

> Allow a man to share his feelings in his own manner. He doesn't always have to be serious to begin with or sit there holding your hands, talking intently about the inner "depth of his being." Some men are more relaxed when they can tell it their way. Allow the man to feel in charge of how he shares his feelings. The way you receive a man's feelings will determine what happens in the future.[3]

Listening is as much a skill as speaking. As you develop your skill of listening he will be encouraged to greater openness regarding the pain and loss he needs to share with you. In their book, *Growing a Great Marriage*, Bob and Emilie Barnes list the following skills of good listening:

• Realize that each of you has a basic need to be listened to.
• Listen intently when your partner is talking to you. Don't just think about your answers. Listening is more than politely waiting your turn to speak.

• Listen objectively. Put down the newspaper, turn off the television, look your partner in the eye, and pay attention.
• Reach out and care about what is being said. Listening is active participation, not passive observance.
• Move past the surface message and get to the heart of what is being said. Listening is more than hearing words.
• Discipline yourself to listen. Listening doesn't come naturally or easily to any of us. Most of us are more comfortable when we are in control and speaking.
• Receive and process the message sent. Try to understand what is being said. At times the message may be painful, but you will be stretched if you continue to listen.[4]

Encouraging Men-Talk

Getting him to talk to you about his losses will be a great help in the healing of his masculine soul. But you're a woman. For all the encouragement and support you can supply, you can't empathize with him like another man can. Somewhere in the process of getting him to talk about his losses he needs to share his burden with other men.

As mentioned earlier, the beginnings of a men's movement in our country has given rise to numbers of men-only support groups and retreats. He needs to find a men's meeting where he can discuss his sense of loss with other men who are carrying the same burden. Some churches are beginning to look at this and are providing groups and periodic retreats and camps. He needs to search out these opportunities for sharing with other men.

The importance of a true mentor in his life cannot be overstated. He will never fully come to peace with his loss of his father until he receives affirmation and validation of his manhood from a substitute father.

Think about It, Talk about It with Him

1. What losses do you feel that your husband is struggling with in the following areas?

    a. Family (including father)

    b. Education

    c. Career

    d. Health

    e. Friendships

    f. Other

2. To what extent is he involved in playing the three roles identified by Joseph Venema in this chapter? For each role, describe evidences you see of his involvement.

    The Solitary Role

Not Involved	Slightly Involved	Moderately Involved	Very Involved	Completely Involved

    The Detached Role

Not Involved	Slightly Involved	Moderately Involved	Very Involved	Completely Involved

    The Success-Machine Role

Not Involved	Slightly Involved	Moderately Involved	Very Involved	Completely Involved

3. What do you think is his attitude about the belief that growth comes through pain and loss? Talk with him about your response.

4. How would you describe his success at talking about his losses?

5. How would you describe your success at learning to listen to him talk about his losses? Talk with him about your response.

6. How would you describe his success at talking with other men about his losses? Talk with him about your response.

11

Living with a Man at Peace

Janice was terrified as she stood at the kitchen window watching Cliff blast their lawn mower with his thirty-aught-six. With each crack of the rifle a new barrage of troubling questions pelted her mind: Has Cliff suddenly snapped and gone crazy? Should I call the police? Should I call our minister? Should I take the children next door and hide out with the neighbor until he cools down? Is this the end of our marriage?

Paying the Price

Fortunately, Janice made some good choices in response to her husband's frighteningly unexpected display of anger.

First, shortly after the incident, Janice mustered her courage to tell Cliff, "Honey, I don't understand why you shot the lawn mower. The whole thing frightens me. If you want to talk

about it, I'm available." Her openness led to conversations between them that gradually uncovered some of the causes of
his anger.

Second, Janice committed herself to help Cliff deal with
his anger. She attended counseling with him, realizing that she
may have been been an unwitting contributor to the smoldering volcano within him that finally erupted when he shot the
lawn mower.

Third, she quietly appointed herself as the ambassador of
health and growth in their relationship and in their home. She
decided that she would do whatever it took to help Cliff take
responsibility for his past and his anger, and to find peace with
himself. She became a constant source of encouragement to
him. She looked for creative ways to affirm his manhood,
competence, and worth. She worked at developing her communication skills so she could talk to Cliff about his emotions
and help him look at his losses. She also took a different role
than before in helping Cliff develop his relationship with his
children, parents, and friends.

An Investment with Dividends

"Is there a payoff for this significant investment?" you ask.
Most certainly—both for him and for you. As for the man in
your life, throughout the book we have used the word *peace* to
describe the desired condition of a man who is coming to terms
with his anger. Walking alongside him will result in his experiencing increasing measures of peace as he comes to terms with
the cultural myths of masculinity, his manhood, his competence, his worth, his past, and his losses—particularly the loss
of his father.

But what about you? You're obviously not in the relationship strictly for what you can get out of it. Like most
women, you're involved with your husband at least as much
to give as to receive. But are there some dividends you can
expect as a result of your investment in helping him?

Yes. First, there is the dividend of what you *don't* receive. In the preceding chapters we have discussed in detail the painful and sometimes tragic fallout of a man's unresolved anger in the lives of his woman and children. By committing yourself to understanding him, you may avert all or most of the destructive consequences that unresolved anger inevitably sparks.

Second, there is the dividend of what you *do* receive: a man at peace. The more he is able to let go of his anger, the easier it will be for him to develop the qualities that will bless and benefit both you and your children. Let's explore some of these qualities.

Priorities in Order

A man at peace is able to put his family first. Having demythologized the ladder-climbing, win-at-all-costs, business-comes-first view of his masculinity, he is free to value wife and children above career and advancement. When he is asked to introduce himself, he may even be able to respond with terms like husband, father, Sunday school teacher, or pack leader ahead of titles like company vice president, salesman of the year, clerk, or lead assembler.

The dividend of his reordered priorities should register significantly in your family calendar. Your husband will likely be home for dinner more often. He'll be more available for family activities and outings. He'll find ways to attend more of your children's ball games, recitals, and school performances and to wrestle with them on the family room floor. And, best of all, he'll have more time for communicating with and courting you.

Family Goals in View

The average man somehow expects wonderful things to happen in his family by magic or through osmosis while he is steering his energies into career goals. But as someone has said, if you don't know where you're going, you'll probably end up somewhere else. The angry man living by the myths of masculinity will plan furiously for success in his career while flying his family by the seat of his pants. And without family goals, such haphazard flight plans often result in a tragic crash.

When your husband is free to strategize the growth and success of his family the way most men strategize the growth and success of a business, the dividends for you and your children may be startling and wonderful. Can you imagine sitting down with your husband to map out your children's college education, design the dream home you will build someday, plan a family vacation or romantic retreat for the two of you, or just to pray together about how God wants you to respond to the needs in your community? Can you visualize organizing your finances together to achieve family goals instead of building a business or soothing frayed nerves or compulsive appetites? When a man is at peace, family goals and achievements take on new meaning.

An Example of True Masculinity

It has been said that children learn much more by what is caught than what is taught. As illustrated in the preceding chapters, the typical man today "caught" and replicated a caricature of masculinity from his hard-driving father. He is today's angry man because the caricature he has adopted has blocked him from having his relational needs met. What's worse, he is passing on to his impressionable children the same skewed example of masculinity.

When your husband finds peace with himself and begins reflecting true masculinity, you and your children will be the beneficiaries. As your sons live with a father who is warm, loving, approachable, and in touch with his emotions, they will learn by example how to be real men. And your daughters will grow up using their father's example as a guideline for establishing dating and marriage relationships with real men. Can you imagine the peace of mind you will enjoy in the years to come as your children enter adulthood having gained a proper view of masculinity from a father who is at peace with himself?

A Figure of Faith

In reality, the concepts, principles, and guidelines for true masculinity presented in this book reflect the precepts of the Bible and the example of the only perfect man in history, Jesus Christ. As a man is helped to relinquish the cultural image of the aggressive, competitive macho man/playboy, he is in a better position to understand God's idea of what a true man is.

This is neither to say that true masculinity is equated with nor required for godliness or righteousness. But as your man comes to peace with himself and his role, he will be better equipped to assume his biblically prescribed role of spiritual leadership and ministry in your home and should choose to follow God's guidelines in this way. Can you think of a better dividend for you and your children?

As you can see, your decision to help your man resolve his anger and find peace is a matter of simple economics. The cost is formidable, but the dividends you and your children will realize far outweigh the investment. Helping your angry man transition into a man at peace is a bargain too good to pass up.

Think about It, Talk about It with Him

1. Complete the following statements in your own words:

The idea of committing my time, effort, creativity, patience, and material resources to helping my man resolve his anger and find peace makes me feel . . .

The idea of realizing personal and family dividends from helping my man makes me feel . . .

2. List the steps toward helping your man you will take or have already begun to take as a result of reading this book.

12

When Men Won't Change

It would be wonderful if we could have provided a money-back guarantee to all women who used the ideas in this book and wound up with an angrier man. We would have guaranteed results if we thought that all men would want to be free from the destructive power of anger. Unfortunately, there are many men who are the way they are and have no desire to alter their behavior or even explore their feelings. They will die angry with the bitter stench of hate still in their mouths.

So what do you do if you find yourself married to, engaged to, or going with a man of intense anger who is unwilling to change or even look at the possibility?Or perhaps the anger is not intense, but you see it there, growing, building, becoming worse with each new irritation. What do you do? We believe you have some decisions to make. Although they are not easy ones, they must be made and made very carefully. These decisions can have effects that last a lifetime.

If you are married and your marriage has been severely damaged over the years by anger, you probably feel very trapped if he refuses to acknowledge the problem. You have prayed and hoped it would go away but it has not. All your dreams of a happy lifetime in a fulfilling marriage are over — you don't dream anymore.

For you there are several options. First, attempt the ideas we have provided previously. Give them time to work. A problem that has developed over years will not be resolved in months or weeks. If you have done anything that has caused a crack in the anger armour, be patient and wait to see if more cracks are coming. You may be unaware that you have started the process of change, and it just needs some time to unfold.

The exception to waiting until your plan has time to work comes when anger has turned to physical abuse and violence. Some would tell you to stay in the midst of the storm, and God will bless you for your commitment. We believe that is short sighted and also very dangerous. You need to protect yourself and your children. Immediate separation is called for when a man becomes physically abusive. When possible, this should be accompanied by a restraining order.

These drastic measures are necessary to break through your husband's denial. He most likely is unaware just how serious his behavior is. He believes his own promises to do better and never hurt again. Separation provides protection, but it also gives the man a dose of reality. The embarrassment and humiliation may lead him to accept the need for change.

There is only one acceptable outcome when a man has reached the point of violence. That outcome is for him to agree to receive counseling. For all you do for him, if he is not willing to give you one hour a week with a counselor, then he has provided you with some valuable information with which to make your decision. Most men resist counseling and just the thought of it motivates them to do better. But when a person has become uncontrollably violent, counseling is the only hope for the development of a normal relationship.

If your angry husband has not become violent and you are not in physical danger, you have some other considerations. You need to be sure that nothing you do is enabling, allowing, or encouraging his state of unhealthy unchange. A good counselor who understands the dynamics of a codependent relationship can assist in altering your behavior and providing support during rough times. Joining a group of Codependents Anonymous is the best way to find healthy support, encouragement, and the confrontation you need to keep you balanced.

In our way of thinking, the question is not whether you should leave your husband, but "How should you stay?" No one should be part of a master-slave marriage where anything outside of a doormat role brings wrath from an angry man. That isn't a relationship; it is an arrangement based on a tainted view of women and an emotionally unstable man. The more counseling and support you obtain from professionals and fellow strugglers, the more likely you will be able to move out of your role as an emotionally abused wife and into a healthy role as an equal partner in marriage.

If you are going with or engaged to a man who is either extremely angry or you see his anger growing, proceed with extreme caution. Do not fall into the trap of believing that you will be able to change him once you are married. Do not become so desperate for a relationship that you settle for living with a tyrant. He won't get better after marriage; he will only get worse. You see his best on this side of marriage. The best foot is being put forward, and if it is an ugly one, do not listen to him or others who would lead you to believe that marriage tames men. If you see danger signs, demand that you both obtain counseling before proceeding further in the relationship. If he won't go before marriage, he is very unlikely to go after marriage, and you will have traded to problem of being single with the problem of an unhappy marriage.

A final word to all women from two men. We men can be real jerks. At times you would think we were trying to be insensitive, uncaring, demanding, and extremely immature. The fact is, most of us are not trying to be that way; we just don't know any other way. Actually, all of those are symptoms of the misery we feel. Most of us want out of those destructive behaviors and we will appreciate your help.

There are some men who are much worse than others. They don't just have a few bad times; they are completely in bad shape. They are not hard to spot. They are surrounded by codependent women who want to tame them or shame them. The sickness of these men attracts the sickness of sick women. If you are one of those, drawn to a man who is destructive and angry, stop and ask yourself why. Ask what needs are being met by being attracted to those who hurt. Resolve those needs, and you will protect yourself from tremendous pain and heartache from a man who does not deserve your companionship.

Whatever your situation, we encourage you to do something you deserve: take care of yourself. Surround yourself with healthy friends who can build you up and even pick you up when things are at their worst. Millions have been helped and taken care of by working the twelve steps and joining a 12-step support group. If one group does not meet your needs, try another one. You will find tremendous hope there.

Another place to take care of yourself is in a loving, caring church. If you are not involved in a church where you are respected and loved, find another one. If you don't attend a church because of something that happened in your past, now is the time to give church another chance. There are many wonderful people who genuinely want to meet your needs.

God bless you as you journey toward wholeness and healthy relationships free of lingering anger.

Notes

Chapter 1

1. Frank Pittman, M.D., "The Masculine Mystique," *Networker*, May/June 1990, 50-51.

Chapter 2

1. Frank Pittman, M.D., "The Masculine Mystique," *Networker*, May/June 1990, 42.
2. David Anthony Forrester, "Myths of Masculinity: Impact upon Men's Health," *Nursing Clinics of North America*, 21, March 1, 1986, 16.
3. Ibid, 18-19.
4. Patrick M. Arnold, S.J., "In Search of the Hero: Masculine Spirituality and Liberal Christianity," *America*, 161, October 7, 1989, 209.
5. Sherry Suib Cohen, "Understanding the Reasons Behind Men's New Sexual Fears," *Glamour*, June 1987, 207.

Chapter 3

1. Ron R. Lee, "After the Revolution," *Marriage Partnership*, Spring 1988, 53.

Chapter 4

1. Karl Bednarik, *The Male in Crisis* (N.Y.: Knops, 1970), 24, 27.

2. David Augsburger, *Caring Enough to Confront* (Ventura, Calif.: Regal Books, 1981), 37.

3. Calvin Miller, "When It's Bad to Be Mad . . . and When It Isn't," *Discipleship Magazine,* 57, 1990, 44.

4. Augsburger, *Caring Enough to Confront,* 41.

Chapter 5

1. Calvin Miller, "When It's Bad to Be Mad . . . and When It Isn't," *Discipleship Magazine,* 57, 1990, 44.

2. Katha Pollitt, "Georgie Porgie Is a Bully," *Time* (special issue on "Women"), November 1990, 24.

3. Carla Rivera and Bill Billiter, "Men Obsessed Can Turn Love into a Tragedy," *Los Angeles Times,* October 29, 1989, section B15.

4. David Anthony Forrester, "Myths of Masculinity: Impact upon Men's Health," *Nursing Clinics of North America,* 21, March 1, 1986, 19.

5. Earl Ubell, "The Deadly Emotions," *Parade Magazine,* February 11, 1990, 4ff.

6. Ibid.

Chapter 6

1. Ron R. Lee, "After the Revolution," *Marriage Partnership,* Spring 1988, 54.

2. Earl Ubell, "The Deadly Emotions," *Parade Magazine,* February 11, 1990, 4ff.

Chapter 8

1. David Anthony Forrester, "Myths of Masculinity: Impact upon Men's Health," *Nursing Clinics of North America,* 21, March 1, 1986, 20.
2. H. Norman Wright, *Understanding the Man in Your Life* (Dallas: Word Publishing, 1987), 126.
3. H. Norman Wright, *Communication: Key to Your Marriage* (Ventura, Calif.: Regal Books, 1974), 55.

Chapter 9

1. H. Norman Wright, *Romancing Your Marriage* (Ventura, Calif.: Regal Books, 1987), 58-62.

Chapter 10

1. Joseph Venema, "Healing the Tear in the Masculine Soul," *The Banner,* September 24, 1990.
2. Ibid.
3. H. Norman Wright, *Understanding the Man in Your Life* (Dallas: Word Publishing, 1987), 1268.
4. Bob and Emilie Barnes, *Growing a Great Marriage* (Eugene, Ore.: Harvest House Publishers, 1988), 114.

STEPHEN F. ARTERBURN is president of New Life Treatment Centers, Inc., providers of alcohol, drug, and psychiatric treatment. He holds degrees from Baylor University and North Texas State University. His books include *Hooked on Life, Growing Up Addicted,* and *How Will I Tell My Mother?* He and his wife, Sandy, reside in Laguna Beach, California.

DAVID A. STOOP is a clinical psychologist in private practice in Newport Beach, California, and is director of the Minirth-Meier-Stoop Clinics. He is also program director of the Minirth Meier Clinic West, a psychiatric treatment program. He holds degrees from Stetson University, Fuller Theological Seminary, and the University of Southern California. His career has seen him in the role of associate pastor and managing editor. His publications include *Hope for the Perfectionist,* and *Self-Talk: Key to Personal Growth.* He and his wife, Jan, have led seminars on personal growth and relationships across the United States and in Australia and France. They are the parents of three sons and have two granddaughters.